The Secret Life of Silent Suffering

When Your Strength Becomes a Prison, Healing Breaks the Chains

CATRINA LABRIE, LPC-S

The Secret Life of Silent Suffering

© 2025 Catrina Labrie. All rights reserved.

No part of this publication may be reproduced, stored in a retrieval system, or transmitted in any form or by any means, electronic, mechanical, photocopying, recording, or otherwise, without prior written permission of the author, except for brief quotations used in reviews or scholarly works.

Published by Catrina Labrie, LPC-S

3126 S Boulevard St. #148

Edmond, OK 73013
United States of America, 2025

ISBN: 979-8-9945425-0-7

This book is intended for informational and reflective purposes only. It is not a substitute for professional therapy, counseling, or medical advice. If you are experiencing emotional distress or mental health challenges, please seek support from a qualified mental health professional.

Printed in the United States of America.

Dedication

This book is a tribute to my childhood Sunday school teacher and mentor, who became a lifelong friend, the one who saw me when I thought no one could. Her belief in me helped begin my healing process. This book will serve as a light for others, just as she was a light for me.

Crystal Heard (and her husband, Michael), thank you for your obedience to God in opening your heart, life, and home to me when I needed it most.

Contents

Why I Wrote This Book 1

Introduction 7

Section 1: Deconstruction
Uncovering the pain beneath the surface

Chapter 1: The Foundation/Blueprint Beneath:
Recognizing the Hidden Struggles That Shape You 13

Chapter 2: The Invisible Architect: How Silent Suffering Quietly
Reshapes Who We Are Becoming 31

Chapter 3: The Hidden Architect:
How Silent Struggles Design Your Life 52

Section 2: Reconstruction
Understanding your inner architecture and beginning to rebuild

Chapter 4: The Unseen Blueprint: The Silent Architect of Your
Emotional World 72

Chapter 5: Silent Foundations: The Architecture of Emotional
Rebuilding 83

Chapter 6: Breaking the Silence as Demolition of Old Structures: The
Trauma of It All 98

Section 3: Strengthening
Building a life of boundaries, resilience, and compassion

Chapter 7: Resilience in the Blueprint:
Designing a Future Built on Strength 120

Chapter 8: Constructing Boundaries:
   Protecting Your Emotional Space 137
Chapter 9: The Invisible Weight of Expectations and the Power of
   Self-Compassion 147

Why I Wrote This Book

Back in 2020, I was reading a blog post from one of my coworkers about silence, and it hit me like a ton of bricks. For the first time, I found words for what I had felt inside for so many years but never could explain. That moment helped me understand the secret life I'd been living; quiet, hidden suffering that no one saw.

I became an expert at wearing a mask, not because I wanted to, but because I didn't know what else to do with everything going on inside me. That hidden struggle, that silent suffering, is what this book is about.

The title The Secret Life of Silent Suffering felt like the only way to name that invisible battle so many of us fight every day.

The Hidden Suffering

I didn't understand it at first, this heavy, quiet thing inside me.
It was like a shadow that never left.
A hollow pain no one could see.
I couldn't explain it, but I felt it crushing me.

I grew up learning that showing emotions was a sign of weakness. No one ever said it out loud, but it was clear in what I saw; the only emotion anyone showed was anger. Don't cry, let alone in public. I thought I was being strong by holding in all those emotions that I felt day after day. It wasn't until I began my journey into adulthood that I discovered it was the opposite of what I thought.

Faith in the Darkness

During that time, I became more vocal about my past and how I felt. My faith grew in this season too, not instantly, but slowly and steadily, like a small light flickering in a dark room. I began to realize that God was not absent in my suffering; He was present in it, weeping with me, walking with me, even when I didn't recognize Him. I began to meet others who had been through similar situations. I wasn't alone! I believe many of you have felt this way or are feeling this way as you read this.

High School Struggles

Years ago, during high school and into my first years of college, I found myself in what I would call an impossible or hopeless situation, secretly deteriorating on the inside. High school years are typically full of late nights, parties, first dates, sports, rebellion, first cars, fun, first loves, preparing for college, and incredible memories that last a lifetime.

However, that is not quite how I remember my high school years. As I reflect on my own experience, a sense of gloom comes to mind. Like many high school students, I suffered from depression. As the years went by, my depression became more intense.

Everything around me seemed to reinforce how I felt inside. Every bad grade felt like proof that I wasn't smart enough. Every lost friendship whispered that I was unworthy. Every rough day at home just added another crack in the foundation I was trying to stand on.

Darkest Moments

I found myself with the constant thought of wanting to commit suicide, daily for years. The only thing I thought I could control was ending everything on my own terms. I was so consumed with my circumstances, and I thought it would've been much easier to leave it all behind. I was sick of feeling worthless and unlovable.

But even in those darkest moments, something deeper inside me whispered that my life wasn't over yet. Looking back, I believe that whisper was God, quiet but constant, reminding me that my story still mattered. That even though I couldn't see the way forward, He could.

Hopeless but Not Alone

How many of us have found ourselves in what we think is a hopeless situation? It is almost as if you get tunnel vision, focusing exclusively on your situation, depression, anxiety, abuse, neglect, etc. Our instinct is to get out of the situation as quickly as possible by whatever means necessary. In pursuing our own solutions to our sinking problems and circumstances, we somehow make everything worse.

Emotional Survival, Not Healing

That season of life laid the foundation for emotional survival, not healing.

It taught me not to challenge my feelings, but to hold them hostage.

To bury anything that looked like weakness.

To never say, "I'm struggling."

And it worked… until it didn't.

Because what you bury doesn't disappear. It just builds.

Layer by layer. Hurt by hurt.

Until one day, you're standing at the edge of yourself with nowhere else to hide.

Breaking the Silence

I carried the thought of ending my life quietly, daily. Not because I wanted to die, but because I didn't know how to keep living. I was tired of pretending. Tired of hiding. Tired of hurting.

My silence had become a prison.

It was during that time that I realized silence wasn't just hurting me, it was keeping me from hearing God's voice. When I finally cried out, it wasn't a fancy prayer, just a broken whisper of "help". And somehow, that was enough. God met me in my most fragile moment and reminded me that even in the silence, He was still speaking.

It wasn't until I finally showed my TRUE self to someone that I found myself on the way to recovery. Breaking the silence is one of the greatest weapons we can use to combat sinking feelings of despair. I thought silence was the answer, but it was actually the fuel keeping my mind in bondage.

The Power of Connection

Making a genuine connection changed the trajectory of my life. That one genuine connection shifted all the years of silent suffering I had endured. That one hug, that one talk, that one prayer, that one word of encouragement, that one pat on the back truly changed my life.

You, my friend, can experience freedom from your silent suffering if you take the step to be vulnerable and make that genuine connection.

Some think it's not very comfortable. No one really cares. I'm supposed to "look" strong. These are a couple of reasons many of us stay stuck. I know I was too embarrassed to share with others; it wasn't something I'd ever done before.

A New Purpose

Becoming a licensed therapist wasn't always my dream or goal. Still, it has evolved into one of my greatest passions, my passion to help others make that connection that will enable them to put an end to their silent suffering. Whether it be from childhood trauma, life's choices, emotional distress, or dreams shattered, it's essential to make that connection! You are not on this journey alone, EVER!

Even if everyone else disappears, God doesn't. Faith has shown me that there is no depth too dark that He cannot reach, no silence too thick that He cannot break through.

This book was written from my heart to help start a conversation, build understanding, and bring awareness to something millions of people may be facing. I encourage you to fully engage with it. Take the time to answer the prompted questions; don't skip them. Let yourself pause, reflect, and be honest with your feelings. For additional resources, tools, and guidance to continue your journey. Remember, this is your story too, and every step you take toward understanding and healing matters.

Rebuilding with Clarity

When disruption shakes the foundation, clarity rebuilds it. Falling apart can be the first step to becoming stronger, clearer, and more authentic.

You are stronger than you know, and brave enough to rebuild.

And with God by your side, you never have to rebuild alone.

Introduction

The Mask of Strength
What if the strongest people you know are silently falling apart? What if that person is you?

Behind every smile, every "I'm fine," there's often a quiet battle no one sees. We've been taught to keep going, to hold it together, to be strong. But strength isn't the absence of struggle; it's often the quiet endurance of pain no one can see.

We wear our strength like armor, unyielding and impenetrable. We hide our cracks, push through the pain, and smile even when we're breaking. But what happens when that armor becomes too heavy to carry? When the weight of silent suffering builds until even the strongest among us feel themselves breaking apart?

Redefining Strength

Here's what I've come to understand: true strength isn't about never breaking. It's about having the courage to break when you need to, to let go of the weight you've been carrying, and to trust that, through vulnerability, you can be rebuilt.

It's about recognizing that the old structure can be torn down and a new one designed stronger, more authentic, and more aligned with who you truly are.

Beneath that armor, there's a truth many of us don't know how to share. A truth buried so deep we sometimes forget it's even there: the truth of silent suffering.

Faith, for me, became the foundation that held me when everything else felt like it was falling apart. It taught me that brokenness is not the end, but the beginning of rebuilding.

How Silent Suffering Shows Up

You might not recognize it at first. It shows up in the quiet moments of exhaustion, the rush to meet others' expectations, or the fear of showing weakness.

Perhaps you've felt an unseen heaviness, or maybe you've been pretending everything's fine for so long that you've forgotten what "fine" truly feels like.

Perhaps it's the quiet ache of unspoken burdens or the overwhelming sense that you've lost touch with the person you once were.

You Are Not Alone

But what if you're not alone in this?

What if the struggles you hide in silence are shared by many, and there's a way to heal, connect, and reclaim your life?

Introduction

It's normal to feel hesitant about questioning whether the weight of fear or shame you carry is valid, or to worry you might be burdening others by sharing it. That hesitation is real.

The world often tells us that vulnerability is weakness and that we must always appear strong. But I want you to know that your struggle matters. Your struggles, no matter how big or small, are essential. The journey through silent suffering doesn't have to be walked alone.

This Book Is for You

Whether you've been quietly suffering for years or are just now realizing that something inside you longs to be heard...

Whether you're a leader who feels the crushing weight of always being "the strong one," a parent who can't bear the thought of appearing weak, or a high achiever who looks successful but feels empty inside, this book is for you.

It's for the caregiver who gives everything but feels invisible.

The creative who pours out beauty while hiding private pain.

The faith leader, the teacher, the student, the spouse, the one who shows up for everyone else but wonders who will show up for them.

If you've ever put on a brave face while falling apart inside, questioned your worth behind closed doors, or carried silent weight so long you forgot what it's like to breathe freely, this book is for you.

This Is Where the Real Work Begins

This isn't just about suffering. It's about reconstruction: how we can rebuild ourselves and find the strength we never realized was within us.

It's about the power of vulnerability, the courage to acknowledge that we're not perfect, but we're enough. It's about redesigning our lives to reflect who we truly are, embracing authenticity, and learning that vulnerability can lead to unimaginable growth.

As we navigate this book, we'll explore how to break through the silence that keeps us isolated, shift the idea that strength means hiding our struggles, and welcome authenticity with open arms.

You'll find practical tools, real-life stories, and encouragement that show healing isn't just possible, it's inevitable.

If you've been silently carrying burdens or wondering how to support someone who does, this book walks alongside you. It serves as a reminder that you're not alone, your struggles matter, and vulnerability can lead to genuine healing.

The truth is that healing begins when we dare to break free from silence and allow ourselves to be seen for who we truly are.

You don't have to stay hidden. You don't have to carry it all alone.

The fact that you're holding this book means something inside you is ready to face the truth, to feel, and to heal.

Introduction

This isn't just my story. It's yours too in the ways you've hurt, the ways you've hoped, and the ways you've kept going.

This is where the real work begins: clarity, purpose, growth.

Section 1

Deconstruction

Uncovering the pain beneath the surface

CHAPTER 1

The Foundation/Blueprint Beneath: Recognizing the Hidden Struggles That Shape You

How Did We Get Here?

In silence, we wear our smiles like armor, concealing the weight of suffering that others cannot see.

Before we can build anything new, we must first understand the foundation beneath us, the hidden layers of silent suffering that support, and sometimes threaten, the entire structure of our lives.

But how did we get here? How did silence become the default way we deal with pain? From a young age, many of us are taught to keep our emotions under wraps. We've heard phrases like *"Stop crying before I give you something to cry about. You're fine, shake it off." "Stop being so sensitive. "Other people have it worse, and there's nothing to be upset about,"* echoed through family rooms and school hallways. These early lessons plant the idea that pain isn't something to be shared openly, but something to be hidden away.

Beyond family, the broader culture around us often teaches us to value strength, productivity, and appearance over vulnerability and authenticity. In a world that applauds business and "pushing through," admitting struggle can feel like failure. The message is clear: keep going, keep smiling, and never let anyone see you falter.

Now, gently ask yourself, have you ever noticed how you respond when you or someone else expresses pain? What messages did you receive about showing vulnerability growing up?

The Collective Sense of Dysfunction

Over the past year, I have been studying a concept known as the collective sense of dysfunction. Silent suffering doesn't happen in isolation. It is part of a larger dysfunction that often weaves into the fabric of our communities, families, and workplaces, not just through obvious problems but also through the unspoken, heavy expectations tied to the roles we play.

Every role, whether a mom, an employee, a pastor, or a student, comes with silent, unvoiced demands about how we are "supposed" to be. These expectations weigh on us, even when no one says them aloud. For example:

- The mom who feels she must always be nurturing, organized, and endlessly patient with-out showing when she's tired or overwhelmed.

- The employee who is expected to be dependable and productive at all times rarely admits stressing or burnout.
- The pastor who carries the weight of being a spiritual guide often feels like they must hold everything together for others while quietly wrestling with their own doubts.
- The student who is supposed to be resilient, capable, and successful, even when anxiety and pressure mount beneath the surface.

These roles come with invisible rules: Don't complain. Don't falter. Don't let others see your cracks. They create a collective atmosphere where vulnerability feels unsafe, and where people silently endure their struggles to avoid disappointing others or losing respect.

This unspoken weight forms a kind of collective dysfunction, where everyone plays their part, but few feel truly seen or supported. The pressure to live up to these silent expectations keeps people isolated in their pain, even as they're surrounded by others doing the same.

I've experienced this myself, feeling the quiet pressure to "have it all together" and to meet expectations without faltering. Whether at work, in community leadership, or within the family, I often found myself pretending to be fine, even when exhaustion and doubt were creeping in. It wasn't until I recognized that many others carry similar silent burdens that I realized how widespread and deeply rooted this collective silence really is.

Understanding this collective dynamic is important because it helps us realize that silent suffering isn't just an individual issue; it's baked into the systems and roles that shape our daily lives. It challenges us to rethink how we support one another and how we create spaces where honesty and vulnerability are not just allowed but encouraged.

Have you felt the silent weight of expectations tied to your role? How does it affect the way you show up in your relationships and responsibilities?

When Silence Speaks Louder Than Words

You might be reading this and thinking, "I don't suffer like this." But silent suffering doesn't always look the way we expect. It often hides in plain sight, wrapped in everyday smiles, busy routines, and polite conversations.

Maybe you don't see it in yourself, but it might be quietly living inside someone you love or encounter every day. Your spouse may be carrying the weight of their own hidden battles, struggling to keep it all together while pretending everything is fine. Your child might be putting on a brave face at school, concealing fears and worries they don't know how to express. The leader who always seems to have the answers may be running on empty after sleepless nights. The employee who smiles through exhaustion and stress could be silently drowning beneath the surface.

Silent suffering is more common than we realize, and often people don't even recognize it until it's named. It thrives in the spaces where pain isn't talked about, where vulnerability is feared, and where "fine" becomes the default answer to every "How are you?"

Think about the people in your life who seem strong, capable, and put-together. Could any of them be carrying silent burdens that you don't know about? And what would it mean if you offered them a little more grace, a little more space to be real?

Why Do We Hide Our Pain?

But why is talking about it so hard? Why do we hide it in the first place? The reasons can be as varied as the people who experience them, and often, they feel like a heavy weight all by themselves.

For some, it's the fear of being judged. We worry that if we open up, people will see us as weak, be disappointed, or worse, treat us differently. Maybe you've asked yourself, "What will they think of me if they knew the truth? What if I'm no longer the person they expected?"

Then there's the shame that often accompanies our struggles. Whether it's feeling like we're failing or falling short of our own standards, shame keeps us trapped in silence. We believe no one else could understand, or that our pain is "too much" for others to handle. You may fear your pain is too messy, inconvenient, or overwhelming for those around you. However, the truth is that everyone carries burdens; some wear them more quietly.

Perhaps it's the desire to protect those we love. We don't want to add to their struggles or weigh them down with our own. So, we stay silent, thinking we're doing the right thing. Yet, in holding back, we often create a deeper distance between ourselves and the people who care.

And then there's that internal voice telling us to be stronger. We tell ourselves we should handle it alone, that admitting struggle means failure. You might feel like you've been the one everyone leans on, providing steady support, so asking for help now feels wrong. But here's the truth: asking for support isn't weakness, it's a courageous step toward healing.

If I can be honest and sum it up, the main reason I stayed silent for so long and sometimes still do is that, deep down, I wondered, "Why does it even matter?"

That thought became the quiet wall between me and healing. When pain feels endless, when your voice feels unheard, or when you've convinced yourself that your story won't change anything, silence can feel easier than hope. But I've learned that your voice does matter. Your story does matter. The moment you begin to believe that truth, even just a little, something begins to shift.

Now, gently ask yourself, which of these reasons feels most familiar to you? Or is there another reason you've discovered that keeps your pain hidden?

The Effects of Silent Suffering

Silent suffering can creep into your life without you even realizing it. You might think that if you keep pushing through, everything will eventually get better on its own. However, the longer you hold onto your inner struggles in silence, the more they can subtly affect various aspects of your life. Your emotions, physical health, relationships, and even how you see yourself.

At first, the signs may seem minor. Perhaps you feel more drained than usual or lose interest in things that once brought you joy. You may not recognize it as silent suffering at first, but over time, these small changes accumulate. You might withdraw more from others or struggle to maintain connections.

Silent suffering doesn't always announce itself with dramatic symptoms; it often works quietly in the background until you realize something isn't quite right.

The Emotional Impact

One of the most common effects is emotional numbness. You might think, "I'm just tired or stressed, it's nothing serious." However, emotional numbness isn't always a complete shutdown. It can be subtle: connection fades, joy feels harder to come by, life feels a bit more distant, and you find yourself just going through the motions.

This emotional distance can creep up slowly, disguised as regular business or stress. But when emotions aren't processed, they don't disappear. They build walls between you and the people you care about.

Chronic Stress and Physical Consequences

The physical effects of silent suffering can sometimes manifest in subtle, unexpected ways. For many people, emotional pain doesn't stay confined to the mind or heart; it can begin to affect the body, too. While experiences vary widely, these are some of the ways chronic emotional stress might show up:

- **Chronic Fatigue:** You might feel drained even after rest. Some people describe a sense of constant tiredness that sleep alone can't fix, possibly the result of carrying unspoken emotional weight.

- **Headaches and Migraines:** Long-term stress is known to contribute to tension in the body, which can trigger headaches or migraines for some.

- **Muscle Tension and Pain:** Unprocessed emotions may contribute to physical discomfort, particularly in the neck, shoulders, back, or jaw. It's not uncommon for people to experience tightness, aches, or general fatigue when under emotional strain.

The Foundation/Blueprint Beneath: Recognizing the Hidden Struggles That Shape You

But what does this look like in everyday life?

It might look like:

- Pushing through your day on autopilot, even when everything in you feels tired.
- Snapping or shutting down emotionally, not because you're angry or cold, but because you're overwhelmed.
- Waking up with a sore jaw or tight shoulders, unsure when you even clenched up.
- Canceling plans, not from disinterest, but from the quiet exhaustion of holding yourself together.
- Struggling to focus, forgetting little things, or feeling like your brain is in a fog.
- Going emotionally numb, functioning on the outside, but feeling disconnected inside.

This isn't about diagnosing or assuming; everyone's body responds to stress differently. But it is about paying attention. These patterns might not always be obvious or dramatic. Often, they build slowly, over time, until they feel normal.

What's important is this: if you've noticed signs like these, it doesn't mean something is wrong with you. It might just mean your body is speaking the truth your mind has been trying to ignore.

Silent suffering, when left unacknowledged, can subtly shape how we navigate the world, mentally, emotionally, and yes, even physically. Listening with compassion is the first step toward understanding what your body, mind, and spirit may be trying to tell you.

Body Awareness Check-In

Sometimes, the body holds onto what the heart hasn't had words for. Take a few quiet minutes and check in with yourself, not to "fix," but to notice.

Find a comfortable position. Take a deep breath in through your nose... and out through your mouth. Again, in... and out.

Now gently ask yourself:

- *Where am I holding tension right now?*
- *What part of my body feels heavy, tired, or tight?*
- *Have I felt rested lately? Or just "on"?*
- *Are there areas in my body that feel ignored or overworked?*
- *What would it look like to give my body kindness, even for a moment?*

You don't need to force answers. Just noticing is enough. Sometimes awareness alone can be a first act of healing.

Try this grounding thought:

I am allowed to rest. I am allowed to feel. My body is not the enemy; it's trying to care for me.

The Emotional Impact

One of the most common effects of silent suffering is emotional numbness, a quiet detachment that slowly takes hold. You might tell yourself, *"I'm just tired... just busy... It's nothing serious."* And maybe it doesn't feel serious at first.

However, emotional numbness isn't always immediately apparent. It doesn't always look like a total shutdown. Sometimes, it's just a quiet drifting away from yourself and the things that used to matter. Joy becomes harder to access. Laughter feels thinner. Life starts to feel like something you're watching instead of living.

You might find yourself going through the motions, showing up, checking boxes, doing what needs to be done, but feeling strangely disconnected from it all. The color fades. The spark dims. And the worst part? You may not even notice it happening until it's been that way for a while.

This kind of emotional distance can creep in gradually, disguised as normal stress, busyness, or burnout. But when emotions aren't processed, they don't disappear; they settle in, creating quiet walls between you and your inner world, and between you and the people you care about.

You may become less patient, more irritable, or overly withdrawn. You may avoid conversations that require emotional presence because you're afraid you won't be able to offer it or even feel it. You may start to wonder why everything feels "off" when nothing seems obviously wrong.

But this disconnection isn't a personal failure. It's often a response to prolonged emotional overload, a subtle defense mechanism that your body and mind use to cope with what feels too heavy to carry fully. Numbness is not the absence of emotion; it's the protection from emotion we don't yet feel safe enough to face.

The good news? If you're noticing this numbness, it means something in you is still alive and paying attention. That noticing is a first step, an opening, toward reconnection, healing, and emotional clarity.

The Myths and Realities of Anxiety and Depression

Anxiety and depression are two of the most common emotional challenges people face today. Yet, despite their widespread presence, there's still considerable confusion and misunderstanding about what they truly mean, how they function, and their impact on our lives.

Let's start with anxiety.

Anxiety is often misunderstood as just "worrying too much" or "being overly nervous." But it's much more complex than that. Anxiety can show up as a persistent feeling of fear or dread, physical symptoms like a racing heart or stomach aches, and even difficulty concentrating or sleeping. It's not just about feeling nervous before a big event; it's a deeper, often chronic state that can affect every part of your life.

One of the biggest myths about anxiety is that it's just "in your head," or that it's something you can "snap out of" if you just try harder. This is far from the truth. Anxiety is rooted in the brain's response to perceived threats, often triggered by a mix of genetics, life experiences, and chemical imbalances. It's not a weakness or a character flaw; it's a real condition that requires understanding and support.

Depression, similarly, is more than just feeling sad. It's a complex mental health condition that affects mood, energy, motivation, and physical health. People with depression might feel hopeless, lose interest in things they used to enjoy, have trouble sleeping or eating, and experience persistent fatigue. Like anxiety, depression is often misunderstood as "just being in a bad mood," but it's a serious condition that affects how a person thinks, feels, and functions.

Another myth about depression is that it's a choice or that someone can "just snap out of it."

Depression involves changes in brain chemistry and function, and while recovery is possible, it often requires treatment, support, and time. It's not about willpower or simply "cheering up."

Anxiety and depression can coexist, and when they do, it can make daily life even more challenging. The stigma around mental health often keeps people from seeking help, leading to prolonged suffering and isolation.

Here are some essential truths to remember:

- *Anxiety and depression are common and treatable.*
- *They are medical conditions, not personal failings.*
- *Seeking help is a sign of strength, not weakness.*
- *Recovery is possible, and you're not alone in this.*

Understanding these myths and realities is a crucial step toward breaking down stigma and creating space for healing. If you or someone you love is struggling with anxiety or depression, know that help is available, and that healing starts with compassion, connection, and courage.

Now, let's look at how anxiety and depression can hide in your daily life, often going unnoticed even by you.

These conditions don't always show up as dramatic or obvious symptoms. For many, they quietly influence how you think, feel, and act in ways that blend into your everyday routines. You might show up at work, take care of family, or socialize with friends, all while carrying an invisible weight.

Anxiety may look like constant second-guessing, feeling on edge without knowing exactly why, or avoiding certain situations out of fear.

You might keep busy to distract yourself or stay late to make sure everything is "perfect" because your mind won't let you rest.

Depression can be even more subtle. It might feel like a dull numbness or a heavy fog, draining your energy and joy. You may find yourself withdrawing from people or losing interest in activities you once loved but still pushing through because you think you have to.

These "functioning" symptoms can be exhausting and isolating. You might hear others say, "But you seem fine," which can make you doubt your own experience. This invisibility often keeps people stuck, afraid to reach out because they don't think their struggles are "serious enough" or worry they'll be misunderstood.

Recognizing how anxiety and depression hide in everyday life is the first step toward seeking support and beginning to heal. You don't have to wait for a crisis to ask for help. Healing starts with acknowledging what you're feeling, even when it's silent and invisible.

The Role of the Therapist in Healing Trauma

As a therapist, I understand the gravity of trauma. I don't just listen to my clients, I also walk alongside them as they face their fears, confront their pain, and slowly begin to heal. It's not always easy. There are often moments when clients hesitate, unsure of whether they're ready to confront the deep-seated hurts they've carried for years. But each step forward is a step toward freedom. Healing trauma requires patience, self-compassion, and a willingness to be vulnerable.

One of the most powerful things we can do for those who carry unhealed trauma is to listen without judgment, offering them a space where their pain is valid and their emotions are heard. This allows them to exhale, knowing they are not alone in their suffering.

The Path to Healing: Finding Connection

Healing doesn't happen in silence. It begins when we take the courageous step of being seen.

For many, the turning point comes when they open up to someone they trust and feel comfortable with. It might feel uncomfortable at first. The inner critic may say, "They won't understand," or "I'm too much." But opening up to a friend, family member, or therapist can lift the weight of silent suffering and begin the healing process.

Sharing your story creates space for healing, not just for you, but for others who may be quietly suffering as well. When you say, "Me too," it breaks the chains of silence and builds connection.

For years, I silently suffered. I believed that by keeping my struggles hidden, I was protecting myself and those around me. But the silence only intensified the burden. It wasn't until I opened up and was met with compassion that I truly began to heal.

Take a deep breath. You're not alone. Your pain doesn't have to be a secret anymore.

Key Insights from Chapter 1

Chapter 1 begins with uncovering the cracks and weaknesses beneath the surface, setting the stage for reconstruction and the creation of new blueprints for connection and strength. Healing starts in the hidden places, the parts of ourselves we've kept quiet, the thoughts we never dared to speak, and the weight we carried while showing up for everyone else.

This chapter exposes the silent struggles that have shaped our foundation, revealing that your suffering is not a failure but evidence of survival. With the blueprint now visible, the careful work of rebuilding stronger supports can begin. This journey asks us to hold space for painful truths, lean into disruptive insights, seek clarity amidst familiar fog, and pursue purposeful growth even when staying the same feels safer.

You do not need to fix everything at once or prove your worth through your pain. What you can do is begin again from a place of honesty and hope. Healing starts quietly, courageously, and completely, and this chapter lays the first stone of that path.

Restorative Reflection

What silent struggles have I accepted as "normal" or "invisible"?

_____

_____

_____

In what ways have I contributed to keeping these parts of myself hidden?

_____

_____

_____

What might change if I allow myself to truly see and acknowledge them?

_____

_____

_____

CHAPTER 2

The Invisible Architect: How Silent Suffering Quietly Reshapes Who We Are Becoming

Not all pain breaks you. Some of it rewrites you, quietly, without asking.

At first, silence feels like shelter. But eventually, it becomes a cage. What starts as protection turns into isolation. The longer we stay quiet, the harder it gets to speak. We forget what it's like to feel seen.

I once asked someone, "Why do you think it's so challenging to talk openly about how we truly feel, especially with the people we love most?" They paused for a moment, then quietly answered, "What good will that do? It'll just make them worry. And we already have enough to worry about."

That answer stuck with me. Not because it was unusual, but because it was so familiar.

It struck me how many of us carry this belief that our pain is somehow a burden, that sharing it will only add weight to the people we love. That silence is the more responsible, more loving choice.

In that moment, I realized that silence isn't always rooted in avoidance or emotional detachment. More often, it's born from love.

A quiet, deeply ingrained belief that protecting others means withholding the truth of our suffering. We think: If I keep it to myself, they'll be okay. If I carry it alone, they won't have to.

But what we fail to see is that the people who love us can feel our silence. They may not know the details, but they sense the distance. The unspoken tension. The emotional weight we're carrying behind the mask.

What starts as an act of care becomes a quiet form of disconnection. And over time, that silence doesn't protect the relationship, it starves it. It keeps the people who love us on the outside, guessing, wondering, feeling helpless.

We think we're sparing them worry, but what we're really denying them the chance to be there for us and denying ourselves the chance to be seen and held.

Silence feels noble. But in the end, it often leaves everyone alone in the dark.

The Internal Toll of Silent Pain

Silence doesn't just shape how we relate to others; it begins to reshape how we relate to ourselves. Over time, we may not even realize how much we've stopped asking ourselves the hard questions: What do I need? How do I really feel?

We become skilled at managing, performing, and enduring, but disconnect from our own inner landscape.

In this state, emotional pain becomes background noise, constant and draining. We carry it in our bodies: tight shoulders, restless sleep, an exhaustion we can't explain. It becomes harder to name what's wrong because we've grown used to not naming it at all.

And perhaps most quietly of all, we lose access to parts of ourselves. Our creativity, our joy, our ability to hope. Not because they're gone, but because they're buried under layers of unspoken pain.

The cost of silence isn't just loneliness. It's self-forgetting.

The Cultural Weight of Silence

This silence isn't always self-imposed. Sometimes, it's culturally taught. We internalize the idea that talking about our pain is burdensome, weak, or attention-seeking.

And when society celebrates those who suppress their emotions and sacrifice their well-being for performance or productivity, it becomes even harder to break the silence.

We see others doing the same masking, performing, and surviving, and we mistake it for normal.

What we're witnessing isn't strength. It's shared dysfunction.

Emotionally, silence amplifies the weight of unspoken pain, causing it to grow until it affects every area of our lives. Physically, it manifests as fatigue, tension, and stress as our bodies absorb the emotional weight we refuse to release.

We convince ourselves that silence protects us, but in truth, it silently consumes us, reshaping who we are becoming in ways that often go unnoticed.

The Justification of Silence: "It's Just Who I Am"

Growing up, I was conditioned to believe that my voice didn't matter. In my household, there was an unspoken rule: children were seen, not heard. Silence wasn't just expected, it was enforced. Any attempt to speak up, question, or express emotion was met with irritation, dismissal, or indifference.

I remember one night, I was maybe six or seven, and I had a nightmare that left me shaken. I tiptoed into the living room, heart racing, hoping for comfort. But instead of arms that wrapped me in reassurance, I got a sharp glance and a cold, "Go back to bed. You're fine."

That was the night I learned that feelings were inconvenient, that my voice was too much.

From then on, I taught myself to disappear without physically leaving. I told myself that being quiet was simply a part of who I was, someone who didn't speak much, someone who preferred to retreat inward rather than engage with the world around me. It felt safer that way. After all, silence meant no one could criticize or reject me. Silence became my armor.

What I didn't realize then is that silence wasn't my personality, it was my protection. A survival strategy. My thoughts, feelings, and experiences weren't always acknowledged, and I internalized the belief that they weren't significant enough to share. I convinced myself that speaking up wasn't necessary. After all, who would care? Who would want to listen? The idea of expressing myself seemed selfish, even foolish.

And so, I kept everything inside.

Over time, this silence didn't just shape how I communicated, but it also shaped who I thought I was. It followed me into adulthood. In conversations, I second-guessed my words. In relationships, I minimized my needs. I avoided confrontation like the plague, not because I lacked opinion or feeling, but because I'd learned that staying silent was the only way to stay safe.

Eventually, though, the silence began to feel less like protection and more like a prison.

I wasn't confronting my pain.

I wasn't processing my emotions.

I wasn't connecting with the people around me.

I had built walls to keep others at a distance, and inside those walls, I was quietly suffocating.

When Silence Becomes Identity

It's easy to confuse emotional suppression with personality. We say, "I'm just private." "I don't like to burden people." "I'm not emotional." But how much of that is truly who we are and how much is who we've had to become to feel safe?

For me, silence had become part of my identity, not because it was natural but because it was necessary.

I called it strength.

I called it being "low maintenance."

I called it humility.

But deep down, I was hiding.

Hiding from rejection.

Hiding from pain.

Hiding from the fear that if people truly heard my voice, saw my needs, or witnessed my truth they'd walk away.

What's Your "Because This Is Who I Am" Story?

The story I just shared is one version of why silence becomes a shield, a habit, a personality. Maybe you've lived something similar, or maybe your silence comes from a different place.

Maybe it was the fear of being called dramatic…

Or the exhaustion of constantly being misunderstood… Or the trauma of never being safe enough to speak. We all have reasons for the silence we carry.

Now, gently ask yourself, what is your "because this is just who I am" story? When did silence become your refuge, and when did it become a cage? How has it shaped the way you show up in the world, in your relationships, and in your faith?

Silence is complex. It's not a weakness, it's survival. But survival is not the same as living.

You were not born to stay small.

You were not created to stay silent.

And that voice you've been tucking away all these years?

It still matters. It always has.

The Subtle Transformation Behind Silent Suffering

Silent suffering is like a slow simmer on the back burner of your life. You don't notice it at first there's no dramatic explosion or sudden change, but gradually, the heat builds, quietly altering the flavor of everything you are. It's a process so gradual that by the time you recognize it, you're not the person you thought you were.

Imagine a pastor, standing before their congregation, offering words of hope and strength. Beneath the steady voice is a simmering weariness, a quiet doubt that no one sees. The weight of countless others' pain, carried silently, reshapes their sense of faith and resilience, sometimes making them question their calling or the very nature of hope itself.

Or consider a business owner, constantly making decisions, leading teams, and pushing forward. They appear confident, unshakable. But inside, silent suffering shifts their priorities, perhaps breeding anxiety or a fear of failure that wasn't there before, changing how they measure success and how much they trust others to share the load.

A parent, who once greeted each day with boundless energy and joy, may find themselves quieter, more cautious, holding back worries and fears to protect their children, while silently grappling with their own exhaustion and grief. Their patience thins, their smiles feel forced, and yet they continue, often unaware of how much the silent weight has reshaped their daily experience.

A nurse or doctor, accustomed to caring for others through crisis, might experience a deep, quiet shift, compassion mingling with burnout, resilience shadowed by silent sorrow. The constant exposure to pain reshapes their worldview, sometimes leaving them emotionally numb or questioning the meaning behind their tireless efforts.

A student, juggling the pressures of education, friendships, and future uncertainty, might carry silent suffering that slows their spark. The slow simmer could show up as self-doubt, fatigue, or a quiet withdrawal, shaping how they see their potential and worth, often without knowing why. What once felt like boundless possibility may feel muted and distant.

A therapist, trained to listen deeply to others' pain, may silently carry their own. The slow simmer of unspoken struggles might reshape their empathy and patience, but also risk emotional exhaustion and blurred boundaries, transforming how they connect with both clients and them. They may question their effectiveness or feel a quiet dissonance between the healer they want to be and the human they are.

And the average working person, the person who clocks in every day, juggles deadlines, family responsibilities, and the endless hum of daily life, may find their silent suffering showing up as fatigue that sleep won't fix, irritability that surprises them, or a quiet sense that something inside has shifted that they can't quite name. The steady grind reshapes their sense of possibility and self-worth, often leaving them wondering if they're doing enough or simply surviving.

This transformation isn't always easy to name. It's not about "getting over" the pain or snapping back to your old self. Instead, it's about becoming a new version of yourself, shaped quietly and persistently by your silent suffering. Your values may shift, your worldview may bend, and your heart may harden or soften in ways you don't immediately understand.

The slow simmer of silent suffering can leave you feeling disconnected from who you once were, but it also opens the door to a deeper, more authentic self. A self-shaped not just by pain, but by the resilience and growth that come from facing the pain, even when it's unseen.

Silence as a Protector and a Prison

Silent suffering often begins as a refuge, a quiet place where we believe our pain will be safe, hidden away from judgment and misunderstanding. At first, silence feels like a shield. It's a protective barrier that keeps others from seeing the raw edges of our struggle. We tell ourselves that if we don't speak about the pain, if we don't expose the cracks in our armor, then maybe we can avoid further hurt or disappointment.

For the person silently suffering, this silence can feel like a necessary survival strategy. It may offer a momentary sense of control, holding the chaos inside without spilling it out. But the truth is, silence is a double-edged sword. While it protects, it also isolates. The pain doesn't disappear; it lingers in the shadows, slowly weaving its way into every thought, every emotion, every interaction.

As time passes, that protective silence can transform into a prison. What once seemed like a safe hiding place begins to confine and constrict. The invisible weight grows heavier, dragging down spirits and clouding minds. It makes it harder to connect, to be honest, even with us. The walls of silence separate us from the very people who might offer support, empathy, or relief.

For those around us, witnessing someone's silent suffering can be confusing and painful in its own way. When someone we love withdraws into silence, it often leaves us feeling helpless and uncertain. We see the signs, maybe subtle changes in mood, quiet withdrawal, or a distant gaze, but without words, it's hard to know how to help. Our efforts to reach out might be met with closed doors or guarded responses, deepening our frustration or sorrow.

The silence, in this way, creates a mutual distance. The person suffering feels isolated and misunderstood, while those who care feel powerless and disconnected. This invisible barrier doesn't just silence pain; it silences relationships, leaving everyone involved feeling alone in different ways.

Emotionally, the silence can feel suffocating. It traps unspoken fears, sadness, and anger, allowing them to fester beneath the surface. Physically, it can manifest as tension, fatigue, or unexplained aches, as the body carries the burden we refuse or cannot express. Spiritually, it may erode hope, leaving a quiet despair that's hard to name.

Yet, this silence isn't always self-imposed. Sometimes it is taught or reinforced by cultural, family, or societal messages that tell us to "be strong," "don't burden others," or "keep your feelings to yourself." These messages convince us that silence is the safer, wiser choice, even when it costs us connection and healing.

Recognizing silence as both protector and prison is the first step toward understanding its complexity. It's not simply "good" or "bad." It's a profoundly human response to suffering, one that deserves compassion for us and for others.

Now, gently ask yourself, where in your life do you hide your pain behind silence? How does that silence defend you, and how might it also trap you? When you witness someone, you care about retreating into silence, what feelings does that bring up in you? How might their silence affect your ability to support or connect with them?

Acknowledging these questions doesn't require answers at this time. It simply opens a small space to begin noticing the impact of silence on your life and relationships.

The Internal Toll of Silent Pain

In this state, emotional pain doesn't roar; it becomes a dull, constant background hum, like static on a radio, always there but easy to ignore. It drains your energy, clouds your clarity, and colors every moment with a shade of exhaustion you can't shake. This pain isn't just in your mind; it lodges in your body. The tightness in your shoulders, the restless tossing at night, the heavy weight on your chest when you try to breathe deeply, all these are silent signals your body sends when your spirit is worn thin.

The ache is real, but nameless, because over time, you've grown used to not naming it. You push it down, tuck it away, hoping that if you ignore it, it will fade. But silence doesn't make pain disappear; it burrows deeper.

The cost of this silence is far greater than loneliness. It's a gradual self-erasure, a waking up one day to a reflection in the mirror that feels unfamiliar, like a stranger staring back. You realize that in protecting yourself with silence, you have slowly lost touch with who you really are.

We tell ourselves silence is protection, a shield against judgment, vulnerability, or rejection. But the truth is far more sobering. Silence doesn't protect; it consumes. It eats away at the spirit piece by piece, reshaping who we are becoming without our awareness. Before long, we're living with shadows of ourselves, fragments of the person we once knew, fragments that whisper of pain, fear, and isolation.

This silent suffering doesn't just live inside; it leaks out into every part of our lives. Relationships become strained; conversations feel like walking on thin ice. You might find yourself withdrawing, unable to fully connect, or pushing loved ones away because the weight feels too heavy to share. Everyday tasks that once felt simple now seem monumental. Getting out of bed, focusing on work, or even smiling feels like climbing a mountain with invisible burdens on your back.

The exhaustion isn't only physical, it's emotional and spiritual. It's a prison built from unspoken words, hidden tears, and the weight of unshared burdens. And the longer it stays locked inside, the harder it becomes to find the key.

For some, the toll of silent suffering may not feel this drastic. The pain might be quieter, more like a faint whisper than a roar. It can be so subtle that it's easy to overlook or dismiss. You might not see how deeply it affects you or even realize you're carrying this weight at all. However, even small, unseen cracks can slowly erode our foundation over time. Whether loud or quiet, the impact of silent pain is real, and it deserves attention and care.

What Being Seen Looks Like in the Midst of Silent Suffering

Being seen is not always about grand gestures or perfect words. In the quiet, complicated space of silent suffering, being seen often looks different for each person. Sometimes it's hard even to know what that looks like. Many people caught in silent pain say, "I don't even know what I need from others." That uncertainty is normal and understandable.

Being seen might mean someone simply sitting quietly with you, offering their presence without pressure or expectation. It could be a gentle question like, "How are you really doing?" without rushing for an answer. Or maybe it's noticing the small changes, the way your eyes shift, the hesitation in your voice, and responding with kindness rather than impatience.

So, what can you do when you don't know exactly what being seen means for you, or when you don't know how to show up for someone silently suffering?

Begin by recognizing that *being seen is about presence, not perfection.* It's about creating space for honest feelings to surface, even if only a little at a time. It's about practicing patience with yourself and others, knowing that healing and connection happen gradually.

If you're the one suffering silently, you might start by tuning into minor signs within yourself. What moments bring relief, what interactions feel safe, what kind of presence feels least threatening? It could be as simple as someone listening without interrupting or someone just being there when words don't come.

If you're witnessing someone's silent suffering, try to show up with gentle curiosity instead of assumptions. Ask open-ended questions, share your willingness to listen, and give permission for silence without rushing to fill it. Remember, your presence is powerful even when no words are spoken.

Ultimately, being seen in silent suffering is a slow, fragile process. It requires courage, patience, and grace from both the one suffering and the one witnessing. It's not about expecting others to understand your pain magically, but about gently opening doors to connection, one small moment at a time.

Instead of searching for the "right" way to be seen or understood by others, it can be healing to begin with gentle, honest questions directed inward, questions that invite you to meet yourself with kindness and curiosity:

- *What feels safe for me right now? Is it simply the quiet presence of someone who sits beside me without judgment or pressure? Is it someone who listens without trying to fix or explain away my pain?*
- *When have I felt truly seen before? What was it about those moments that made me feel understood or accepted? Was it the way someone held space for my story? The absence of rushing or interruption? Or simply the feeling that I mattered, just as I was?*
- *What fears arise when I consider opening up or being vulnerable? Are there worries about being judged, rejected, or misunderstood? How might those fears influence what I ask for, or what I hesitate to ask for, in moments of need?*
- *What small, simple acts of connection or kindness have made me feel less alone? Perhaps it was a smile from a stranger, a gentle touch on the shoulder, a word of encouragement, or a moment of shared silence. What do those moments teach me about what I truly need from others?*

Exploring these questions isn't about rushing toward neat answers or checking off a list. It's about creating a sacred space within yourself, a space where you can begin to understand what presence, compassion, and understanding genuinely means to you, in your own time and on your own terms. This inner exploration honors the complexity of your experience and lays a foundation for an authentic connection that feels safe and healing.

The more I stayed silent, the more isolated I felt. The silence became a justification, a way to avoid vulnerability and the discomfort of exposing my true self. It was easier to keep everything hidden than to risk being judged or misunderstood. But in doing so, I lost the opportunity to connect with others, to be seen and understood. I lost the chance to let my pain be heard.

Over time, I realized that silence wasn't an inherent part of who I was. It was a learned behavior, a result of years of feeling unheard, unseen, and unimportant. My journey toward healing began when I finally accepted that my voice mattered. That my feelings and experiences deserved to be shared, not hidden away. Only then did I begin to understand the power of breaking the silence.

The "They Should Already Know" Trap

One of the most frustrating parts of silent suffering for both those who suffer and those who witness is the expectation that "they should already know."

For the person silently struggling, this can mean feeling invisible or misunderstood, as if their pain is obvious but simply being ignored. They might think, "If they really cared, they would just understand." Yet, silent suffering by its very nature hides beneath the surface, wrapped in silence and often subtle behaviors. It's not always obvious to others, even those closest to us.

For the people around them, it can feel confusing or hurtful. They might think, "I'm right here, why aren't they telling me what's wrong?" or "If they need help, why don't they just ask?" This expectation that others should intuitively know creates a frustrating loop where nobody feels truly understood.

The truth is that silent suffering doesn't come with clear instructions or signals. Everyone carries their pain differently. No one can read minds or feelings, no matter how close the relationship. That's why breaking the silence when it feels safe is so crucial.

Instead of assuming others should already know what you're going through, consider that most people want to help but don't know how. And instead of expecting someone silently suffering to speak up perfectly, recognize that it's a process of building trust, patience, and small moments of being seen.

This shared misunderstanding can keep people trapped in silence longer, but it also opens the door to compassion both for yourself and for others. We're all doing the best we can with the tools and awareness we have. Healing starts when we move beyond assumptions and start creating space for honest, gentle communication.

The Courage to Break Silence

Breaking the silence is never easy. It takes courage to reveal what we've hidden, especially when we've convinced ourselves for so long that our pain is too heavy to share or that others won't understand. But breaking the silence is also the first step toward reclaiming our voice, our identity, and our connection to others.

When we finally speak, it's not about oversharing or forcing ourselves to be vulnerable before we're ready. It's about opening a small door a crack where light can enter, where healing can begin. It's about allowing someone to witness our truth, even if it's imperfect, messy, or incomplete.

I remember the first time I broke my silence with someone I trusted. My voice shook. The words stumbled out awkwardly. But as I spoke, something inside me shifted. The burden of carrying pain alone began to lift, and for the first time in a long time, I felt seen.

Reclaiming Our Identity

As we break the silence and share our suffering, we begin to reclaim the parts of ourselves that silent pain tried to erase. We rediscover our voice, our feelings, and our worth. We realize that suffering doesn't define us, but it does shape us, and that's okay.

Through this process, we move from surviving to living. From hiding to showing up. From isolation to connection.

Our silent suffering becomes a source of strength, wisdom, and authenticity, not a mark of shame.

Key Insights from Chapter 2

Chapter 2 explores the weight of unspoken pain and its profound impact on our lives. Carrying hidden struggles is like holding a heavy, invisible burden; what begins as fleeting discomfort can gradually build into overwhelming tension. The mental and physical toll of keeping pain inside is enormous, draining energy, distracting us, and even affecting our bodies. Unspoken pain creates barriers not only between us and others but within ourselves, fostering fear of judgment, rejection, or misunderstanding.

Silence, rather than protecting us, traps us in isolation and deepens disconnection from the parts of ourselves that most need healing. Healing begins when we stop carrying that burden alone. Breaking the silence, though difficult, opens the door to connection, relief, and strength. Vulnerability, even in small acts, becomes the foundation for recovery.

There is no shame in suffering, asking for help, or taking the time to heal. By embracing our pain, sharing it with trusted others, and giving ourselves grace, we move toward a future where the burden of silence no longer defines us. You are worthy of peace, connection, and healing. The silence that once trapped you is not the end; it is the beginning of your journey toward wholeness.

Restorative Reflection

What unspoken pains have I kept locked inside?

_____

_____

_____

What would it mean for me to share even a small piece of this pain, either with someone I trust or with myself?

_____

_____

_____

CHAPTER 3

The Hidden Architect: How Silent Struggles Design Your Life

What we hide becomes what we carry, and it gets heavier with time.

Shame is not an isolated event, but a quiet, insidious companion that follows us through life. It's not something we consciously invite in; it's something we learn to live with. Over time, it becomes part of the foundation of who we think we are, silently weaving itself into our thoughts, actions, and relationships.

Shame isn't always loud. It doesn't always announce itself with an overwhelming sense of guilt or sorrow. It doesn't shout; instead, it whispers. It's the voice in your head that says, "You're not good enough," or "You're not worthy of love." It lingers. It slides into your thoughts, shaping your decisions in ways you may not even notice. It becomes your quiet but ever-present companion, dictating how you interact with the world and, most painfully, how you view yourself.

Shame is a silent sufferer. It doesn't cry out for help. It doesn't break down in public. Instead, it quietly lives inside behind smiles, behind accomplishments, behind the masks we wear. It is the invisible burden carried alone, the weight felt in moments of solitude, the quiet voice that never stops telling us we're not enough.

The Mask of Perfection: Why We Hide

Think about the high-achieving student in college. They've mastered the art of looking successful. Perfect grades, a social life that appears effortless, and leadership roles that others admire. But behind this polished exterior is a crippling fear of failure. Every accomplishment feels like a way to prove to themselves that they are, in fact, worthy. They work relentlessly because, at their core, they believe that if people knew the real them, if they knew the anxiety, the loneliness, the fear, they would be rejected.

This isn't just a passing thought; it's the silent narrative that runs under the surface. The mask of success becomes an armor to protect against the vulnerable parts of themselves they fear others might judge. Each "I'm fine," they say to friends, is a little lie they tell to shield the truth: They feel like they're barely holding it all together.

Then consider the mother who seems to have it all figured out. Her kids are fed, safe, and loved, but on the inside, she's exhausted. The weight of parenting, the expectations of society, and the constant comparison to other "perfect moms" have worn her down. She keeps a smile on her face because that's what is expected. But behind closed doors, she questions herself. When the stress finally boils over, and she raises her voice in frustration, she's consumed with guilt. Shame tells her she's failing. "You're not as good as everyone thinks you are," it whispers.

She doesn't talk about it. She doesn't admit how close to the edge she feels. Instead, she keeps trying to maintain the perfect image, the socially acceptable one. She plays the role of "mom" rather than showing her authentic, vulnerable self. But this performance is not sustainable.

Both examples illustrate a key point: shame thrives in the spaces we refuse to acknowledge. It lives in the parts of us that are hidden away, tucked into the corners of our hearts that we hope no one will notice. The more we try to hide, the stronger it becomes.

The Hidden Scars of Our Past: How Wounds Shape Us

The scars we carry aren't signs of brokenness; they're evidence of survival and strength.

Shame often has deep roots in our past. These roots are planted in moments when we were too young to defend ourselves, too vulnerable to understand the full weight of what was happening. They take shape in unspoken words, emotional neglect, and actions that leave lasting marks on our hearts. These invisible scars aren't always easy to spot, but they shape the lens through which we view ourselves and the world around us.

Think about a young child whose feelings were dismissed. "You're too sensitive" or "Boys don't cry." These words aren't just hurtful in the moment; they begin to form the foundation of beliefs that will guide how this person sees themselves for years to come. As they grow, they may internalize the belief that emotions are something to hide, that sensitivity is a flaw, and that love and acceptance must be earned through strength or achievement.

As an adult, this belief shows up in subtle ways. Perhaps they're emotionally distant from their spouse, afraid to show vulnerability because it feels like a sign of weakness. Maybe they push themselves to the point of exhaustion at work, fearing that if they take a break or show signs of struggling, they'll be seen as incapable. The mask of perfectionism is not a choice; it's a defense mechanism built from years of trying to survive the emotional neglect and rejection they felt growing up.

The Healing Journey: From Performance to Presence

Healing doesn't come from pretending the past never hurt you. It means choosing to stop letting the past define your future.

To heal, we need to be willing to sit with the discomfort of our scars. This isn't easy. It requires a shift, a willingness to open what we've kept locked away, to give voice to the pain we've kept hidden. This is where the real work begins: embracing vulnerability.

Vulnerability is often seen as a weakness. But in truth, it's the greatest strength we can offer ourselves and others. When we stop performing and start being present, when we allow ourselves to be imperfect, we create space for others to do the same. This is where true connection happens.

For instance, consider the executive who has spent years hiding behind success. She's built a fortress of achievement to protect herself from the shame that tells her she's not good enough. But what if, instead of constantly striving to be perfect, she allowed herself to be human? What if she could say, "I struggle too"? What would happen if we stopped performing and started being honest? Would the world collapse? Or would we find that our honesty creates space for others to heal as well?

The shift doesn't happen overnight, but it starts with one simple act. Saying, "I'm struggling" to a friend, a therapist, or even to ourselves. This act of sharing, of being seen, is a sacred step toward freedom.

The Power of Compassion: Embracing Your Imperfections

When you begin to open up, it's essential to approach yourself with compassion. This means speaking to yourself the way you would talk to a dear friend, with kindness, understanding, and gentleness. So often we judge ourselves harshly, holding ourselves to an unrealistic standard of perfection. But the truth is that your imperfections are not what make you unworthy; they make you human.

Start with awareness, notice when shame arises. When do you feel small or unworthy? What triggers that internal voice that tells you, "You're not enough"? By simply noticing these moments, you take the first step toward reclaiming your power.

The next step is compassion treat yourself like you would someone you love deeply. When shame tells you you're not worthy, answer it with kindness. Remind yourself that you are enough just as you are.

And finally, embrace connection. Find safe spaces where you can be seen and heard. Healing happens in community, and you are never alone in your struggle.

You Are More Than Your Shame

Your past mistakes or hidden scars do not define you.

You are more than your achievements, more than your failures. You are a beloved child of God, worthy of grace, healing, and belonging.

When you stop hiding and start being real, you open the door to something incredible: freedom. Freedom from the weight of shame and the ability to step into the fullness of who you were always meant to be.

The Road to Freedom

The road to freedom begins with one truth: You don't have to be perfect to be loved. You don't have to perform to be worthy. You are enough right now, just as you are.

As you continue on this journey of healing, remember that every scar, every imperfection, is a mark of survival. They are proof that you've made it through the toughest of times.

Your story is still unfolding, and it's not one of perfection. It's one of grace, growth, and courage. You are worthy of all the love and connection you've been afraid to claim.

The Bandages of Our Past: Shame and the Hidden Scars

The scars we carry aren't signs of brokenness; they're evidence of survival and strength.

Shame doesn't just appear out of nowhere.

It often grows quietly, seeded in the wounds of our past. The unspoken moments, the unmet needs, the silent heartbreaks. Childhood trauma, emotional neglect, rejection, abandonment, betrayal all of these can leave invisible scars that stay with us far longer than we realize. Scars that shape how we see ourselves, how we relate to others, and how we move through the world.

As children, we're especially vulnerable. The harsh words of a parent, being dismissed when we needed support, or subtle messages like "you're too sensitive," or "stop crying, be strong," become embedded in our identity. They don't pass; they take root. And as we grow, those painful moments start turning into deeply held beliefs: I'm not good enough. I don't matter. I have to be perfect to be loved.

Think about a father in his forties raising two kids, working hard to break generational cycles. But deep down, he's haunted by the emotional absence of his own father. He never heard, "I'm proud of you." Now, even though he tells his children he loves them, he struggles to believe he's doing a good job. Every mistake feels like proof that he's failing not just as a parent, but as a person.

That's the voice of shame inherited, internalized, and deeply ingrained.

Many of us learn to cover our scars with achievement, performance, or perfection. We build polished lives, craft strong images, and master the art of having it all together. But inside, we're often weighed down by self-doubt and a relentless need to prove our worth. We believe that if we can just stay in control, if we're productive, attractive, spiritual, or successful enough, we won't have to feel the ache of what's buried underneath.

But the pain doesn't go away just because we dress it up. We may suppress it, but it leaks out in our relationships, our choices, our stress, our silence.

She's a high-achieving executive with a corner office and accolades. But no one sees the little girl inside who was constantly told, "You'll never be good enough." So now she works twice as hard as everyone else, trying to outrun the echo of that lie. She can't rest because rest feels like failure. Vulnerability terrifies her because what if someone sees that she's not as confident as she seems?

Her productivity is a mask, not because she's manipulative, but because she's protecting a part of her that still feels unworthy.

We don't need to hide our scars; they are the badges of our survival.

But shame tells us the opposite. Shame says if people saw the real you the parts that are anxious, angry, lonely, or afraid they'd reject you. So, we hide. We isolate. We push people away before they can get too close.

And those scars? Instead of honoring them, we treat them like defects. We cover them with perfectionism. We numb them with addiction, avoidance, or endless business. Not because we're weak, but because we're scared.

He's a pastor, counselor, and mentor. He teaches about grace every week but has never told anyone about his struggle with anxiety. Growing up, emotions were seen as lack of faith, so he learned to bottle everything up. He prays, leads, and loves others, yet quietly wonders, if they knew I wrestled with this, would they still trust me?

He wears a spiritual mask not to deceive others, but to survive in a world that doesn't always make room for leaders to be human.

We often believe that healing means forgetting what happened or moving on. But healing doesn't mean pretending the past never hurt you. It means choosing to stop letting the past define your future. It's the sacred act of saying: yes, I've been hurt. But I am still here. And that matters.

In truth, our scars don't make us less, they make us more. More compassionate. More self-aware. More human.

Your imperfections don't make you less worthy; they make you real.

We all carry stories of loss, failure, or fear. But when we embrace our imperfections instead of hiding them, we create space for authentic connection. We realize we're not alone, and that is where healing begins.

A Biblical Reminder: Power in Weakness

In a world that prizes strength, success, and self-sufficiency, vulnerability is often misunderstood as a flaw to be hidden, a weakness to overcome. But the gospel turns that narrative completely upside down.

The Apostle Paul's words in 2 Corinthians 12:9 offer one of the most powerful insights into God's heart toward our brokenness:

"But he said to me, 'My grace is sufficient for you, for my power is made perfect in weakness.' Therefore, I will boast all the more gladly of my weaknesses, so that the power of Christ may rest upon me."

Paul's honesty here is revolutionary. He doesn't pretend to have it all together. He doesn't rely on his own strength or image. Instead, he embraces his weakness, and in doing so, he becomes a vessel for God's power.

This reveals a life-changing truth: *God's strength doesn't require our perfection, just our surrender.*

When we stop performing and pretending, when we admit we're tired, broken, or overwhelmed, we make space for God's power to do what our own strength never could. It's not the polished version of us He wants to use; it's the raw, real version, the one with scars, doubts, and questions.

Think about the paradox: Our weakness isn't a barrier to God; it's the entry point. It's the space where His grace shows up most visibly. This isn't just spiritual theory; it's something believers across generations have experienced firsthand. In their lowest, most vulnerable places, *God's grace was not only present, but it was also enough.*

The idea that "power is made perfect in weakness" also calls us to radical authenticity. It invites us to stop hiding behind competence, control, or a curated image of strength. God doesn't ask us to be impressive. He asks us to be present. Fully present, with all that we are, not just what we think is acceptable.

He doesn't meet us in our perfection. He meets us in our pain.

You don't need to be "fixed" to be found by God. You don't have to clean yourself up before you approach Him. His power doesn't wait on your strength; *it meets you in your surrender. In your silence. In your shame. In your exhaustion.*

"He gives strength to the weary and increases the power of the weak."
Isaiah 40:29

In fact, God delights in using our weaknesses as a canvas for His glory. When we lean into His grace instead of our image, we become living testimonies of His love, mercy, and transformation.

So instead of hiding your scars, shrinking from your struggles, or waiting until you feel strong, remember this: your weakness is not a disqualification. It's an invitation.

Let go of the pressure to "look okay." Embrace the freedom of being fully known, fully loved, and fully empowered by grace. That's where actual strength lives.

Take a few quiet moments to reflect on this:

Where in your life do you feel the need to appear strong? And what might it look like to invite God into that weakness instead?

Write honestly. There's no need to filter or fix your thoughts. This is your space to bring your whole, authentic self, questions, fears, doubts, and all, before God. Let this be a moment of surrender, not performance.

Prayer Starter:

God, I don't always know how to let go of the need to be strong. But today, I invite you into the places where I feel weak, ashamed, or tired. Help me trust that Your grace is enough, even in this place. Amen.

The Turning Point: Speaking Our Truth

"Shame cannot survive being spoken. It cannot survive empathy."
-Brené Brown

Shame is a silent, suffocating presence when it stays locked inside. But the moment we give it voice, whether through a journal entry, a prayer, a therapy session, or a trusted conversation, something powerful shifts.

When you say out loud, "This is what I've been carrying," you break the silence that shame depends on. You shine a light on the shadows, and in that exposure, shame loses its grip.

Examples of Speaking Truth

Some carry their struggles with anxiety or self-doubt silently for years. When they finally share their story with a trusted friend, the burden often feels lighter. Compassion replaces judgment, and the realization grows that they are not alone in their pain.

Others might find relief in writing a letter to God in their journal to confess feelings of inadequacy. In that honest moment of prayer, a deep peace can arise, a reminder of God's unchanging love and perfect grace for imperfect people.

This is the turning point, the sacred moment when the heavy burden begins to lift and healing quietly takes root. Speaking your truth doesn't erase the pain instantly, but it cracks open a space where vulnerability can grow.

The Bible encourages us to bring our burdens into the light. Psalm 34:18 reminds us, "The Lord is close to the brokenhearted and saves those who are crushed in spirit." When we speak our truth in prayer or confession, we invite God's healing presence into our pain.

Finding Safe Spaces to Speak

Finding the right space to speak your truth is essential. This might be:

- A trusted friend who listens without judgment.
- A counselor or therapist trained to provide support.
- A spiritual mentor or pastor who offers guidance rooted in faith.
- A support group where shared experiences foster understanding.

These safe spaces create environments where empathy can flourish, where shame's voice is silenced by kindness and acceptance.

The act of speaking our truth is not just a step in healing; it is the doorway to transformation where shame is replaced by grace, isolation by community, and silence by authentic connection.

Why Speaking Your Truth Matters

- Because someone else is waiting to hear your story.
- Because your silence is heavy, and healing is light.

- Because freedom doesn't begin with perfection; it begins with honesty.

When we speak the truth, even just "I'm struggling," we give ourselves permission to be fully human. We invite grace into the places we've kept guarded.

Your truth is not too heavy for love. It's not too dark for light. It's not too messy for healing.

The Weight We Carry: How Shame Shapes Our Stories

Shame isn't just an emotion; it's a story we tell ourselves about who we are.

It whispers that we are less than, flawed, unlovable, broken. These stories get tangled into every part of our lives, influencing how we think, feel, and behave.

It can make us shrink back when we want to step forward. It can make us lash out when we feel cornered. It can make us hide when we want to be seen.

These stories are often unconscious. We don't always realize they are running the show.

For example, you might find yourself pushing people away just as things get close, not because you don't want connection, but because deep down you believe you're not worthy of it.

Or you might overwork yourself, believing your value depends on what you produce or achieve.

Or you might numb your feelings with substances, distractions, or business to avoid facing the painful parts inside.

These behaviors aren't about being selfish or weak; they're about trying to survive shame's heavy weight.

The good news is that these stories can be rewritten. You don't have to carry shame's narrative forever.

Breaking the Cycle: Steps Toward Freedom

The first step is awareness.

Start noticing when shame shows up, when you feel small, unworthy, or scared to be seen.

Name it. Give it a voice.

The second step is compassion.

Treat yourself like you would a dear friend. Speak kindly to your inner child. Remind yourself that you are worthy of love, just as you are.

The third step is connection.

Find safe people to share your story with, people who will listen without judgment and remind you that you're not alone.

Healing happens in community.

The fourth step is faith.

Remember that your value is not tied to your performance or perfection. You are deeply loved by God, exactly as you are.

Lean into that truth.

You Are More Than Your Shame

You are not defined by your past mistakes or hidden scars.

You are not your failures or the voices in your head that tell you otherwise.

You are a beloved child of God, worthy of grace, healing, and belonging.

The road to freedom starts with speaking your truth.

It continues with choosing to love over fear.

It grows when you allow yourself to be seen, fully and authentically.

You don't have to hide anymore.

Your story matters.

And the world needs the real you.

Now, gently ask yourself, what does "enough" feel like to you? How can you remind yourself that you are imperfect, but whole and enough, every day?

Key Insights from Chapter 3

Chapter 3 emphasizes that healing from shame is not a single moment or destination, but a continuous journey. It is a process in which you learn to embrace vulnerability, confront unconscious patterns that have shaped your life, and offer yourself the same compassion you would extend to others. You are not defined by your mistakes or the things you have hidden. Each step you take in letting go of shame brings you closer to reclaiming your true self, your worth, and your inherent power.

Your scars, whether emotional or physical, are not burdens; they are symbols of resilience, proof of your ability to face hardship and continue moving forward. Healing does not come from perfection, but from the courage to show up as you are, with all your imperfections and scars.

You do not need to be flawless to be worthy of love, connection, or peace. The journey begins with self-acceptance, and when you stop allowing shame to define your story, you reclaim control and start writing a new chapter filled with compassion, self-forgiveness, and understanding that you are enough exactly as you are, right now. You are worthy. You are loved.

You are never alone on this journey, and healing is happening every time you honor yourself, flaws and all. The story you are meant to live is just beginning, and it is beautiful. Embrace it with an open heart.

Restorative Reflection

What feelings or thoughts come up when you consider speaking your truth about your struggles?

_____

_____

_____

How might giving voice to your pain change the way you see yourself or your situation?

_____

_____

_____

What fears or doubts hold you back from being vulnerable with others?

_____

_____

_____

Section 2

Reconstruction

Understanding your inner architecture and beginning to rebuild

CHAPTER 4

The Unseen Blueprint:
The Silent Architect of Your Emotional World

Just because you carry it well doesn't mean it isn't heavy.

The Silent Storm

For many who suffer quietly, the storm is not a sudden downpour or a heart-racing thunderclap. Instead, it is a slow, unrelenting drizzle that seeps into every corner of life, almost invisible from the outside. You may not feel like you are falling apart or losing control. Rather, you feel as if you are trapped in a haze, a fog that dulls your senses and muffles your emotions. Days blend into one another, not because you are tired or sad in the usual way, but because you are carrying a quiet weight that no one can see.

It feels like living under a heavy sky that never clears. You move through your days performing routines, smiling, nodding, pretending. All the while, the storm hums quietly in the background. No one hears it, because it does not scream. It simply exists, steady and persistent.

You might not even recognize it as suffering because it becomes your "normal." You forget what it feels like to be truly free or light. The exhaustion is real, but it is the kind that sleep cannot fix. You feel disconnected from yourself, from others, and from hope.

This silent storm is isolating. It builds walls that keep others out, not because you want to push them away, but because you lack the energy or the words to let anyone in. Slowly, day by day, the silence grows, deepening the divide.

This is the reality of silent suffering. It is not always visible. It is not always loud. But it is real, and it deserves to be seen.

I have carried my own silent storms for years. There were moments when the weight was so subtle that no one around me had a clue. I would wake up feeling a fog that made everything seem distant, even the things and people I loved most. Not because I was sad in a typical way, but because I was stuck beneath a quiet gray sky that never lifted.

There were days when I went through the motions perfectly, smiling, talking, making plans, while inside, the storm whispered softly but relentlessly. I thought this was just how life was supposed to feel.

Sometimes friends would ask how I was, and I would say "I'm fine," not because I believed it, but because the silence felt safer than trying to explain the unexplainable. Opening up seemed too risky, too vulnerable.

One of the hardest parts was feeling disconnected, like watching life through a glass wall. I was close enough to see the joy, but too far to touch it. I felt isolated even when surrounded by people, trapped by the very storm I carried quietly.

- *Can you identify moments in your life where the storm felt more like a quiet drizzle than a thunderous downpour?*

- *Have you ever found yourself feeling "normal" amidst exhaustion or numbness? What did that feel like?*

- *Are there walls you have built around your pain that might be quietly separating you from others?*

- *How might it feel to start lowering those walls, even just a little? What does healing look like to you in the context of this silent storm?*

The Weight of Quiet Loneliness

There is another kind of loneliness, one that sneaks up on you. I used to try to prove to myself that I did not need anyone else. I could, in fact, do life alone. I did not come from a loving family that was always present and walked through life together. So, I learned that only I could take care of myself well. That was, until I encountered God. He quickly drained every single lie and piece of brokenness out of me.

This kind of loneliness is different; it doesn't arrive loudly. It does not knock or announce itself. Instead, it creeps in quietly, settling in the corners of your life, until one day you realize it has been there for a while. You do not remember when it arrived. It just became part of you. It seeps into your routines, conversations, and silences. And you carry it like a weighted blanket.

There were times I did not even recognize it as loneliness. I told myself I was just tired. Just busy. Just focused. But deep down, I was disconnected from others. From myself. I convinced myself I did not need anyone, that I was stronger on my own. That if I could make it through the day, the week, the season, I would be okay.

Have you ever found yourself carrying that quiet loneliness without even realizing it? That silent companion that clings to your daily steps but never speaks a word. Maybe you thought you were just being independent or resilient, but beneath that strength, there was a part of you longing for connection, for someone to truly see you, to walk with you through the storm.

The silence can feel safer than vulnerability, but over time, it becomes its own prison. The more you carry it alone, the harder it becomes to reach out and to break the cycle.

What would it look like to acknowledge this loneliness? To sit with it without judgment and invite someone in? Because sometimes, the storm does not have to rage in silence anymore.

But survival is not the same as being okay.

You can be surrounded by people laughing, talking, working, and even loved, and still feel the ache of isolation. It is not always about the absence of company. Sometimes it is about the lack of connection. The kind of connection where you feel seen, understood, and held, not because you had to perform for it, but because you showed up as you really are.

Loneliness does not always come from being alone. Sometimes it is the result of hiding the parts of you that are too scared to be rejected. You stop reaching out. You stop sharing the truth. Little by little, silence becomes your default. It feels safer that way. But safety and fulfillment are not the same thing.

There is no shame in silence. We learn it young. We practice it daily. But you deserve more than quiet survival. You deserve connection. And even if it starts with a whisper, even if it feels awkward or messy, you are allowed to speak. You are allowed to be seen.

Have you ever mistaken your silence for strength? When was the last time you felt truly seen? What part of yourself have you kept hidden in order to feel safe? Write it out. Let it rise to the surface just for you, just for now. That is how reconnection begins.

The more you keep to yourself, the more isolated you become. While this might feel like safety at first, it slowly becomes a prison.

Have you ever told yourself that you are sparing others from the emotional weight? Perhaps you tell yourself you don't want to make them uncomfortable or add to their problems. But what if, in reality, you are closing off the one thing that could genuinely help you: connection?

This silence is not always self-imposed. As we know, sometimes it is learned, passed down in subtle, unspoken ways. Maybe you grew up in an environment where emotions were not talked about, where vulnerability was seen as weakness, or where love was offered only when you performed or behaved a certain way. So, you learned to hold it in, not because you wanted to but because that was the only way you knew how to feel safe. That kind of silence gets wired deep. And as adults, we carry it with us, still believing that keeping quiet is the safest path.

You are keeping yourself in emotional isolation, and over time, that loneliness becomes a quiet, gnawing presence. Have you ever felt like no one truly sees you? Here is the truth: you are not allowing anyone to see you.

Think about how this plays out in relationships. Have you ever been in a friendship or partnership, and the other person senses something is off? They might ask, "Are you okay?" But instead of opening up, you shrug it off. "Yeah, I'm fine." Inside, a storm of emotions, hurt, fear, and confusion, rages that you are not sharing. The person asking does not push, believing you because you have always been the one who seems to have it all together. And just like that, the conversation ends. Your silence and your emotions remain beneath the surface.

Perhaps you even know the truth that you want to connect with. You want someone to hear you and to help make sense of it all. But there is a fear that if you let people in too much, they will see something they do not like or will not know how to handle. You feel ashamed of your vulnerability, so you hide it, even from those who love you most.

There are moments when you might feel resentment or frustration toward the people around you for not showing up for your pain when you have not given them permission to do so.

In these moments, silence feels like a shield. It is a way to protect yourself from rejection, misunderstanding, or pity. But here lies the trap: the very act of shielding yourself by keeping everything locked inside prevents you from experiencing the healing power of real connection. Without the courage to open up, you cannot allow others to show up for you. In turn, you remain stuck in a silent struggle that no one even knows you are fighting.

I have been there too, pretending everything is fine when it is not. I have told myself that I did not need anyone's help. Each time I did that, the walls between the people around me and me grew just a little higher. But the truth I have learned is that isolation does not protect us. It makes the pain worse. The more we shut people out, the more we convince ourselves that no one really cares or that no one would understand. In that place of isolation, healing feels impossible.

The Unseen Cost of Silence

The more you keep your struggles to yourself, the more isolated you become. But over time, this silence comes at a high cost not just for you but for the people in your life as well.

It can affect coworkers who notice you withdrawing or seeming distant, but don't know what's really going on. Your children might sense your emotional distance, though you don't talk about it, leaving them unsure or confused. Employers might see a drop in your focus or engagement but miss the silent struggle beneath the surface. Ministries or community groups may feel your absence or quiet pullback without fully understanding why.

These small, quiet shifts can build up over time. By holding everything inside, you unintentionally build walls that separate you from connection and healing. Others may feel shut out, and you may miss the comfort and strength that come from being truly seen and supported. The silence becomes a barrier that keeps not only your pain but also the possibility of shared healing at bay.

No one is meant to carry heavy burdens alone. The cost of silence is high. It dims your spirit, deepens your loneliness, and can strain the very relationships that could help you heal. Recognizing this cost, even in its subtle forms, is the first step toward breaking free from isolation and inviting connection back into your life.

The Role of Compassion for Yourself

Silent suffering often carries with it a hidden burden of self-judgment. Many people internalize the quiet weight they carry as a personal failure, believing they should be stronger, tougher, or more resilient. They might think that if they just tried harder, pushed through more, or "got over it," the storm would lift. But this mindset only adds layers of pain and isolation.

True healing begins when you start extending the same compassion to yourself that you might offer a dear friend. Self-compassion means recognizing that your suffering is real and valid, and that it's okay to struggle without shame or blame. It means allowing yourself space to feel, to be imperfect, and to rest without guilt. This kindness toward yourself creates a foundation from which healing can grow, slowly and steadily.

When you practice self-compassion, you soften the walls you've built, not to expose vulnerability as weakness, but to embrace it as part of your humanity. It's a gentle invitation to acknowledge your pain without judgment and to care for yourself with patience and grace. In this way, self-compassion becomes a powerful tool, not just for surviving the silent storm but for transforming it.

Now, gently ask yourself, how might anxiety or depression be showing up

in your daily life? Are there ways you might be hiding your struggles, even

from yourself? What small signs or patterns do you notice that could be

clues to the silent storm you're carrying? How might your life change if

you began acknowledging these feelings more openly?

Remember, healing is a journey, not a destination. It doesn't require perfection or immediate transformation. It requires courage, honesty, and a willingness to face the silent storms within. You're not alone on this path. And with each step, you're moving closer to the light beyond the clouds.

Key Insights from Chapter 4

Chapter 4 frames you as both the architect and the building, emphasizing that healing is not something that happens to us, but a process in which we actively participate. It encourages taking ownership of your reconstruction, brick by brick, truth by truth. Silent suffering often doesn't look like sadness or panic; it can manifest as numbness, normalcy, or functioning on autopilot. Many of us build emotional walls to protect ourselves, not realizing that these walls also shut others out.

Functioning anxiety and depression can hide behind achievement, responsibility, and even moments of joy. Loneliness may go unrecognized until it becomes a part of your daily life. Resentment can grow when we expect others to show up for pain we have never voiced.

True healing begins with honesty with us and with those around us. You do not need to prove your strength by pretending you don't need anyone; acknowledging your needs is part of genuine reconstruction.

Restorative Reflection

What small, intentional step can you take today to begin building a bridge, either toward healing within yourself or toward connecting with someone else who might be silently struggling?

_____

_____

_____

Take a moment to reflect on how you can become both the architect of your own emotional rebuilding and find opportunity for connection in someone else's life.

_____

_____

_____

CHAPTER 5

Silent Foundations: The Architecture of Emotional Rebuilding

Just because you're functioning doesn't mean you're fine.

The Quiet Weight We Don't Always See

Hope is a paradox, isn't it? It's so easy to talk about hope when life is moving smoothly, and everything feels like it's on track. When the days are light and things seem to be working, hope flows naturally. But what about those moments when everything feels like it's falling apart? What about when it feels like you're carrying the weight of the world on your shoulders and every step forward demands more energy than you have left to give? I've been there too.

Maybe you are in a place right now where hope feels distant or even entirely out of reach. Perhaps you're facing a situation that seems impossible to fix or change. Maybe you're walking through a season of loss, whether it's the loss of a loved one, the end of a relationship, the loss of a job, or the loss of security and stability you once had. Maybe you've been battling an illness that refuses to let go or dealing with a relationship that feels fractured beyond repair. And in the middle of all of that, hope feels like a distant memory or a dream that belongs to someone else.

I want you to hear this and let it sink in. Hope does not always arrive in the way we expect it to. Sometimes it shows up invisibly, like the warmth of the sun that you can't see because it is hidden behind thick clouds. You might feel trapped in the storm unable to see the light, but just because you can't see it doesn't mean it isn't there. Hope is still present. It's quietly waiting for you to look up again and remember that it exists.

Maybe on the outside everything looks fine. You're functioning. You're getting things done. You're leading well, showing up for others, meeting deadlines, caring for your family, and fulfilling every role. You're the parent who keeps the household running even when you're exhausted. You're the business owner who keeps making tough decisions. You're the student meeting everyone's expectations. You're the ministry leader holding space for everyone else's pain. You're the helper, the caretaker, the strong one, and you've learned how to perform strength so well that no one sees how much it's costing you.

The truth is, being seen as "okay" in everyone else's eyes can feel like a prison when you're secretly unraveling inside.

There is a heavy pressure that comes with being the person others depend on. People expect you to be steady. Your children expect you to be calm. Your spouse expects you to be strong. Your church, your employer, your community, your team, they all look to you for answers, for guidance, for direction. And most days, you rise to the occasion.

But what no one sees is the cost of continuing to show up when you're barely holding it together.

You carry the weight of others' expectations as if it's your personal responsibility to hold the whole world together. You smile because you feel like you're supposed to. You keep showing up because you think you have no other choice. And somewhere in the middle of it all, you start to disappear beneath the performance of being fine.

But let me say this to you as clearly as possible:

You are allowed to need support.

You are allowed to feel exhausted.

You are allowed not to have it all figured out.

Being strong does not mean never struggling. Real strength includes telling the truth about how you're really doing. It includes asking for help. It includes taking a deep breath, whispering to someone you trust that you can't do this alone, and allowing yourself to be human again.

Hope shows up even for the ones who look the strongest. Even for the ones who are always the caretakers. Even for the ones who hold space for everyone else. Even for the leaders. Even for you. You do not have to crash in order to reach for hope.

You do not have to earn rest by proving your worth. You do not have to collapse to deserve care. You do not have to hide your heaviness just because others expect you to carry lightness.

You can still be the incredible person you are. The parent. The leader. The student. The giver. The dreamer. And still say the words, "I'm not okay." That admission does not make you weak. It makes you honest. And honesty is what sets you free.

So, take a moment right now. Just breathe. Lay down the pressure. Even if it's only for a minute. You don't have to hold everything together today. Let hope to carry you for once.

I understand that feeling of hopelessness far too well. When hope feels unreachable, it's easy to fall into a spiral of self-blame. You might think things like, "I should have more faith," or "I should be stronger by now," or "Why can't I just handle this better?" You may feel like you're failing simply because you don't experience hope the way other people seem to. But I want to tell you with as much gentleness as possible: you are not failing.

It is okay to not have it all together. It is okay to feel overwhelmed. It is okay to feel lost. Hope is not a test you are trying to pass. It's not about doing everything right. It's about simply continuing to show up, even if you feel broken.

Sometimes hope doesn't come like lightning or a breakthrough moment. Sometimes it shows up in the quietest places. Hope looks like getting out of bed when you feel like staying under the covers. It seems like replying to a text message when you don't feel like talking. It looks like letting yourself cry, even just a little. Or taking a moment to breathe. Or deciding to try again tomorrow. Those small, quiet decisions are hope in motion.

Maybe you're saying to yourself, "I just can't keep going." Maybe it feels like the weight you're carrying is too heavy to hold any longer. But I want you to consider something: hope often grows in the places where everything feels dark. It takes root in your pain like a seed buried deep in the ground. And though you may not see it sprouting yet, that seed is still alive. Still waiting. Still becoming something new.

You do not stumble across hope by accident. Hope is something you choose to nurture. Even when your heart feels weary. Even when you can't see the outcome. It's like planting a seed in cold soil. You may not see growth today or tomorrow. But every act of faith, every breath, every tiny step forward waters that seed. And eventually, you will see it grow.

Even when hope feels far away, remember it doesn't always shout. Sometimes it whispers, sometimes it hides in the quiet moments. And even when it feels invisible, it's still there, just beneath the surface.

It might be pausing for a moment of stillness between meetings, giving yourself permission to rest even when the to-do list feels endless, or quietly acknowledging that you're doing the best you can, even when it doesn't feel like enough.

For me, hope shows up in taking small, baby steps each day, nothing extravagant, just tiny moves forward. It could be as simple as getting out of bed when it's hard, reaching out to one person, or permitting yourself to rest without guilt.

Hope isn't about big leaps or instant fixes. It's about those small, steady steps that add up over time, reminding you that progress is possible, even when it feels slow or unseen.

Please do not let shame convince you that you're not worthy of hope. Do not let guilt persuade you that you're broken because you don't feel hopeful right now. The fact that you feel fragile does not mean you've failed. It means you're human. And sometimes it's in our most tender places that hope begins to grow again.

So, I want to leave you with this truth. Hope is not only a feeling. It is also an act of faith. And sometimes the smallest act, choosing to breathe, choosing to trust, choosing to take the next step, is enough to carry you through the darkness.

You are not alone. Even if it feels that way right now, you are not abandoned in your struggle. Hope is still with you. And it will continue to show up, even in the smallest, most unexpected ways.

Maybe you're not in complete despair, but something still doesn't feel right. Perhaps you're not drowning, but you still feel off-balance. You're not lost in total darkness, but something still feels heavy. Perhaps you're moving through life, doing all the right things, checking the boxes, and showing up, but it still feels hollow. You feel disconnected. There is an ache, and you can't explain it.

If you feel like you're living without truly connecting to your own life, you are not alone. That does not make you broken. It makes you human. Sometimes life doesn't give us a clear sign to tell us exactly what's wrong. We just know that something doesn't feel quite right. We brush it off. We tell ourselves we're just busy. We tell ourselves we're just tired. But what if that ache is trying to tell you something? What if it's a signal that something deeper needs attention?

You may have built walls to survive. But what if those same walls are keeping you from fully living?

You might tell yourself, "I'll get through it," and keep going. But the silence you feel inside? The quiet pressure that follows you into every room? That's not something to ignore. It's real. And it's worth paying attention to.

If you feel stuck, do not dismiss it. Do not minimize your pain. That ache you feel is not a sign of weakness. It's a message. It's your soul asking for care, asking for connection, asking for change.

When you allow yourself to stop pretending and finally face the truth of how you feel whether it's sadness, confusion, numbness, or quiet despair, you create space for healing. You begin to give yourself the same grace you give to others. You begin to permit yourself to be simply.

I understand it can be terrifying to be vulnerable. To admit you don't have it all together. But that honesty is the doorway to becoming whole again. You do not have to be perfect to deserve love, support, or hope.

Take a Moment to Reflect

What parts of yourself have you been hiding to keep things "together" for everyone else?

Have you been showing up in your life wearing a mask of strength while quietly unraveling beneath the surface? Have you put your needs on hold because it feels like there's no space for your own pain? You're not weak for needing support. You're human. And those hidden parts of you? They deserve light too.

Where in your life have you been showing up strong, even though you're running on empty?

Are you pouring out energy in places where no one sees how drained you really are? Have you been the one holding everyone else up while feeling like no one is holding you? Acknowledging your exhaustion doesn't make you less; it makes you real.

How would it feel to let someone in, just a little, to say "I'm struggling" without shame?

Imagine the weight that could be lifted if you didn't have to carry this alone. Vulnerability can feel terrifying, primarily when you're known as the strong one. But honesty is where intimacy begins. It's where relief lives. You don't need to open up to everyone, but what if you chose just one safe person?

What kind of support do you wish someone would offer you right now? Be honest with yourself. Is it a listening ear? Practical help? Encouragement without fixing? Write it down. Name it. You deserve the kind of care you so willingly offer to others.

Are you allowing yourself the same compassion and care you offer to others? You would never speak to someone you love the way you speak to yourself in your most critical moments. So, what would it look like to extend grace toward yourself to talk to yourself with softness, patience, and love?

Let this reflection be a place where truth meets grace, where the pressure to be perfect is replaced with permission to be whole.

You don't need to fix everything today.

You don't need to have the right words.

You don't need a flawless plan.

You don't need to hold it all together for everyone.

You just need to tell the truth, even if that truth is whispered in silence, even if it's only spoken within your own heart.

Take a breath.

Feel your feet on the ground.

Feel your heart still beating.

You are here.

And that is enough.

You're not failing.

You're healing.

And healing begins with honesty with yourself, with others, and with the parts of your story that are still learning how to be seen.

This is the space where people often lose hope.

They look at everything that feels broken in their lives and try to fix it all at once. They make a list, they push themselves, they give everything they've got to "get it together." And when the weight of that proves too heavy, when they realize they can't fix everything overnight, they give up. They walk away. Not just from the process, but sometimes from relationships, goals, dreams, faith, and even themselves.

This is the breaking point not because people are weak, but because they're exhausted. They're overwhelmed by the pressure to be whole in an instant. And when instant healing doesn't happen, they assume it never will.

But hear this: *you don't have to have it all figured out today.*

It's okay to feel lost.

It's okay to be tired.

It's okay to need time.

It's okay to need help.

These moments of uncertainty are *not evidence of your failure*. They are sacred pauses holy invitations to breathe, to slow down, to gently return to yourself. They are reminders that you are not a machine. You are a living, breathing soul worthy of tenderness, worthy of rest, worthy of room to unravel and begin again.

You are not behind.

You are not too much.

You are not running out of time.

You are becoming, right here in this in-between space, even if it doesn't feel like it yet.

But remember this:

You are not required to stay stuck.

You are not sentenced to remain disconnected or alone.

Even when the path ahead feels unclear, even when you cannot see the next chapter, hope is still waiting softly, quietly just beneath the surface.

You don't need to leap.

You just need to take the next small step.

That one small step is an act of faith.

And faith, in the smallest form, is enough.

For example…

Perhaps today, your relationships feel strained, and you're unsure how to repair them. But today, what if you chose to take one tiny risk? Maybe it's reaching out. Maybe it's listening a little longer. Perhaps it's offering forgiveness or asking for it.

Maybe your work or purpose feels blurry. You don't have to make a huge career change overnight. But could you name one thing that brings you curiosity again? Could you make space for joy, even in five quiet minutes?

Hope doesn't demand perfection. It doesn't show up all at once. It shows up in progress, in presence, and in the quiet courage to try again.

Even in confusion, you are not without direction. You are not stuck forever. You are simply in motion in your own time, in your own way.

If you are in the darkness right now, remember:

You are not alone.

Your pain does not disqualify you.

Your exhaustion does not make you less than.

Your hidden struggles do not make you invisible to the One who sees all.

Even if your hope only looks like getting out of bed.

Even if your strength today is found in brushing your teeth or answering a single text message.

Even if your biggest win today is just being here, that is enough.

You do not have to prove your pain to deserve healing.

You do not have to perform your brokenness to earn compassion.

Your silent struggles matter.

They have shaped you.

They have revealed strength in you.

They have softened you, deepened you, prepared you.

You are not broken beyond repair.

You are in process.

You are becoming.

And even in the quiet, you are growing.

Key Insights from Chapter 5

Chapter 5 highlights the dangers of trying to fix everything at once, which can often lead to burnout and hopelessness. When we attempt to solve every problem simultaneously, it is easy to become overwhelmed and feel tempted to give up, but giving up is not always a sign of weakness. Sometimes it is simply a natural response to the impossible expectations we place on ourselves. Feeling lost, tired, or unsure is not failure; these moments are sacred invitations to pause, reflect, and reconnect with what truly matters.

We do not need to earn rest or prove our worth through constant striving. As human beings, we deserve care, compassion, and the space to grow at our own pace. True progress is not always loud or obvious. Often, the most powerful growth occurs in the quiet, unseen moments when we choose to keep going.

Taking a break does not mean we have quit, and needing time or help does not mean we are broken; these are signs of wisdom, not weakness. Healing is not about rushing to the finish line; it is about honoring where we are, even in the midst of uncertainty.

Restorative Reflection

What moments of despair have I faced where I felt completely lost?

_____

_____

_____

In those times, what strengths did I discover within myself that helped me survive and move forward?

_____

_____

_____

CHAPTER 6

Breaking the Silence as Demolition of Old Structures: The Trauma of It All

Unhealed Trauma Isn't Just Painful, It's Controlling

"The body keeps the score."—**Bessel van der Kolk**

Trauma isn't just an emotional or psychological wound; it manifests in the body, in our behaviors, and the way we perceive the world. It's more than just the painful events we've endured; it's the way those events continue to shape our lives long after they've occurred. Whether from family dynamics, failed relationships, betrayals, or career setbacks, unhealed trauma creates a foundation of resistance that prevents us from truly moving forward.

As a trauma therapist, I've seen firsthand how this resistance manifests. People are afraid to open up about their pain, scared to confront the wounds that have shaped them. The silence is not merely avoidance; it is a defense mechanism, a way to protect themselves from the fear that talking about it will either make it worse or expose them as weak or broken. And the longer the silence persists, the more it controls their lives.

The Silent Suffering of Trauma

Trauma is often a silent struggle you may not even realize is happening. For many, the trauma stays buried in the subconscious, covered by daily routines, coping strategies, or the false belief that they should just "move on" or "get over it." Trauma can become a permanent background hum in your life, a constant low-level anxiety that you've learned to live with. And this is the dangerous part: the longer it stays unaddressed, the more it becomes embedded in your identity.

What often happens is that people, especially those who have been through repeated trauma, start to distrust their own emotions. They feel as though their pain is a burden on others or that they shouldn't be feeling so "sensitive" or "weak." They begin to internalize the message that something is wrong with them for struggling. As a result, they push their pain down, bury it deep, and pretend to be fine. They become experts at hiding their hurt, convincing themselves and others that they are "strong."

But this silence doesn't lead to healing. Instead, it feeds the trauma.

The Pressure of Always Being "On"

In today's hyper-connected world, technology has made us constantly available, whether we like it or not. We're bombarded with notifications, emails, and messages from work, family, and social media, all day, every day. While this can make us feel more productive and connected, it can also have an insidious effect on our mental and emotional well-being, especially for those dealing with trauma.

Constant Availability and the Erosion of Personal Boundaries

Whether you're a busy professional, a parent, a caregiver, or a leader, the pressure to be "on" at all times is overwhelming. Technology blurs the lines between work and home, between professional obligations and personal life. You may feel you have to respond to every email, text, or work-related request immediately, no matter the time of day or night.

The result is a steady stream of demands that erodes your ability to rest, recharge, and attend to your own needs. Even when you physically step away from work, your mind remains tethered to your devices, constantly scanning for the next email or text. The boundary between "working" and "living" becomes non-existent, and emotional recovery becomes impossible. This constant engagement is exhausting, both mentally and emotionally, and it often exacerbates the trauma that people are already carrying.

The Emotional Toll of Digital Overload

For those silently struggling with trauma, the pressure to stay constantly connected can be especially damaging. Trauma often leaves individuals feeling like they need to be "perfect" or constantly "on" in order to avoid rejection or judgment. The more someone feels they need to perform or prove their worth, the harder it becomes to turn off. This creates a cycle of constant engagement, where the individual is always running on empty but feels unable to stop.

Technology, for many, becomes a means of self-validation. A response to an email or a like on a post can briefly makes us feel seen and valued. But these fleeting moments of connection don't provide real emotional relief. Instead, they reinforce the pressure to stay "on," always striving for external validation, never allowing themselves the space to heal or to be simply.

The Fear of Being Out of the Loop

In professional roles, especially for leaders, business owners, or pastors, the fear of being out of touch can be overwhelming. There's a subtle but powerful pressure to always know what's happening, to always be available for a crisis, or to offer immediate responses to every situation. In the digital age, "absence" often feels like neglect, and the fear of falling behind, of being "out of the loop," can create a sense of urgency that overrides your need for self-care.

For many people, not responding quickly enough or being unavailable is perceived as unprofessional or uncaring. This fear, whether it's real or perceived, keeps people locked in a state of constant readiness, always prepared for the next request or crisis. It's not just about the work itself; it's about how our identity is tied to our availability.

Emotional Recovery Is Stifled

Emotional recovery requires space to process feelings, space to decompress, and space to rest. But when you're always "on," those spaces are nearly impossible to find. Without rest, the emotional toll of trauma, past or present, becomes a heavier burden. Instead of allowing yourself to process, grieve, or heal, you stay busy, distracted, and constantly in "survival mode."

When we're in "survival mode," we don't allow ourselves the time to confront our pain. We bury it under the noise of our day-to-day tasks and responsibilities. But trauma doesn't disappear by ignoring it. In fact, it often gets louder, especially when it's continually suppressed.

The Burnout Trap

Over time, this constant pressure to be "on" leads to burnout. As a therapist, I've seen this pattern many times. Clients come to me feeling drained, emotionally spent, and overwhelmed, sometimes without understanding why. They've been running on fumes for months, trying to meet the needs of others while performing at a high level, all while completely neglecting their own emotional well-being. And when they finally hit a wall, they feel broken, disconnected, and incapable of continuing at the pace they've set for themselves.

This burnout doesn't just affect work performance; it also impacts relationships, mental health, and overall life satisfaction. If you're caught in the cycle of constant availability, it's challenging to form meaningful connections or experience genuine joy. You're simply surviving, not living.

The Need for Boundaries in the Digital Age

The first step toward healing in the age of constant connectivity is setting boundaries. Boundaries aren't just about saying "no" to others; they're about saying "yes" to yourself and saying yes to emotional recovery, saying yes to rest, and saying yes to your own mental and physical health. Without boundaries, there's no way to create the space needed for healing to take place.

As technology continues to dominate our lives, we must actively reclaim control over our time and energy. That might mean turning off notifications during certain hours, setting specific times to check emails, or simply telling people that you are unavailable after a particular time. It's important to recognize that setting boundaries in this digital world isn't a luxury; it's a necessity for your well-being.

Now, gently ask yourself, have you ever felt the pressure to always be "on"? How does that pressure show up in your life, whether in your job, your family roles, or your personal life? What would it feel like to step back and create intentional boundaries around your time and energy? How can you begin to reclaim your space and honor your need for emotional recovery?

Why the Silence? The Fear of Facing the Pain

One of the most significant barriers to healing is the fear of reliving the pain. Trauma survivors often fear that talking about their experiences will make them too vulnerable, too exposed. This fear stems from a deep-seated need for self-protection. It's easier to stay silent than risk reopening old wounds. This resistance is a natural response to the overwhelming emotions trauma can evoke, emotions that have often been dismissed, ignored, or invalidated in the past.

For many, the fear is rooted in shame. Shame often keeps trauma survivors stuck in the silence, convincing us that we are broken or undeserving of help. Shame tells us we are flawed for feeling the way we do, and in that, it keeps us from reaching out to others for support. The voice of shame is loud and convincing: "If they really knew what you've been through, they wouldn't accept you. You're too much to handle. You don't deserve love or healing."

This belief is toxic, and it's the primary source of resistance that keeps so many from starting their journey toward healing. Shame convinces us that speaking our truth will bring rejection, invalidation, or shame. In reality, sharing our truth is often the key to initiating the healing process.

The Power of Naming the Trauma

Naming the trauma is an incredibly mighty step in breaking the silence. By giving pain a name, you bring it out of the shadows, where it has power over you, and into the light. Naming trauma doesn't make it worse; it makes it real, and in making it real, you can begin to address it.

Trauma doesn't always look how we expect. It is broad, layered, and often misunderstood. Many things can be considered traumatic, and here are just a few we'll mention throughout this book. Trauma can stem from a single shocking event, like an accident or assault, or from long-term experiences such as emotional neglect, childhood abuse, racism, or the chronic stress of living in survival mode.

It can come from growing up in a home where love had conditions, where you had to earn your worth, or where you were the "strong one" who wasn't allowed to fall apart. Some trauma hides in high achievement, people-pleasing, or perfectionism. Some of it looks like silence never being heard, seen, or believed. Some trauma is visible and loud; other kinds are quiet, private, and easily dismissed even by the person carrying it.

Whether it came from what was done to you or what you needed but never received, all trauma is valid. Naming it isn't about comparison; it's about recognition.

When you begin to label your experience, you shift from being passive, allowing the trauma to define you, to being active, taking the first step in regaining control over your story. It's not about reliving the pain for the sake of reliving it, it's about acknowledging that you were hurt, that the trauma exists, and that you are worthy of healing.

Naming your pain is an act of courage. It's an acknowledgment that you have been through something significant and that it's okay to feel what you feel. For some, this can feel like breaking the silence for the first time. It's saying, "This hurt matters. I matter." And it's in that first acknowledgment that the healing journey begins.

As much as I guide others to navigate their struggles, I have had to face my own. For years, I didn't recognize how much my past trauma was affecting my mind, body, and relationships. In fact, there were times when I didn't even realize it was trauma I was carrying. I thought I was just "toughing it out" or that the constant low-level anxiety and physical tension in my body were just a regular part of life.

Trauma and suffering as Silent Forces of Change

We often think of trauma as a sudden, shattering moment, a crash, a wound, a fracture that breaks us in two. And yes, sometimes it is that. But there's another kind of trauma, quieter, slower, almost invisible. It's not a sharp crack, but a deep reshaping, a soft erosion that works beneath the surface, changing the very ground we stand on without us noticing at first.

Silent suffering is this hidden force. It doesn't announce itself with chaos or crisis. Instead, it moves in the shadows, weaving its way through the fibers of who we are. It is the invisible architect of transformation, rebuilding us piece-by-piece while we go on believing we are still the same.

And here's the thing. Transformation is not about going back. It's not a return to some old version of us or reclaiming a life before the pain came. It's about becoming someone new. Someone who carries the marks of suffering, yes, but also the strength and depth that can only come from enduring the invisible.

This shift can be so subtle that it takes years to recognize. Maybe our priorities change. What once seemed urgent now fades into the background. Our values rearrange quietly, like the slow turning of the seasons. Our sense of who we are bends and curves in ways we can't always explain.

Sometimes, the change feels like losing parts of ourselves. The easy laughter, the boundless hope, the sense of safety we never realized was fragile. But if we look deeper, we find that something else is growing beneath the surface: resilience, wisdom, a fierce kind of authenticity.

Silent suffering reshapes us not by breaking us, but by rewriting the script of our lives in ways that only reveal themselves over time. It is the evolution of the soul through the fire of pain, a process that asks us to accept the new shape of our identity, even when it's unfamiliar, even when it's hard.

Trauma Became an Unconscious Force in My Life

Before becoming a therapist, I didn't realize how deeply trauma was affecting me. It wasn't something I consciously acknowledged, but looking back, I can see how it shaped every part of my life. I was carrying emotional weight, unseen and unspoken, and it wasn't until years later that I recognized it for what it was: trauma.

At the time, I just thought I was doing what I had to do. I was strong, resilient, managing life and responsibilities, but somewhere deep down, I was disconnected from my true self. The constant sense of unease, the physical tension, the emotional numbness, these things felt normal, but they were actually signs that something deeper was at play.

It wasn't until I hit a breaking point that I realized how much I had been suppressing. I was trying to push through life pretending everything was fine, but in reality, the trauma I hadn't named yet was quietly dictating my actions, my thoughts, and my interactions with others. It affected my health, my relationships, and even my professional life. That moment of realization was both painful and liberating.

I began to understand that the "strength" I had prided myself on, this ability to hold it together, to be there for everyone else, was really a way of surviving, not thriving. I was walking through life with my emotional wounds unacknowledged, avoiding the pain rather than confronting it. But when I finally faced it, when I understood that my trauma wasn't just an isolated event but a recurring, unconscious force, everything began to change.

This journey of self-discovery didn't just inform my personal healing; it ultimately led me to become a therapist. I wanted to help others who, like me, had been silently navigating the weight of their own unhealed wounds. Because I now knew the power of naming trauma, of bringing it out from the shadows to the light, and I wanted to guide others to do the same.

The Resistance to Seeking Help

As a trauma therapist, I've seen that one of the most challenging hurdles for trauma survivors to overcome is seeking help. Many clients, especially men, professionals, or leaders, feel that they can't show weakness. The idea of asking for support feels like a vulnerability they can't afford, especially if they've spent years holding everything together for others. The fear of being judged, of being seen as inadequate or incapable, often outweighs the desire for help.

This resistance is not a sign of weakness, though; it's a sign of the internalized pressure to be strong and perfect. It's a reflection of the societal and familial expectations placed on them. And the longer the silence continues, the harder it becomes to ask for help.

But it's important to remember that asking for help is not a sign of weakness; it's a sign of incredible strength. It's an acknowledgment that healing cannot be done alone, and that you are worthy of support and care.

The Trauma in Families and Relationships

Family trauma can be especially insidious. When you grow up in an environment that's unstable, where emotional needs are not met, or where you were taught to "suck it up" and not show vulnerability, it becomes incredibly difficult to break free from those learned behaviors.

In family systems, trauma is often perpetuated because we don't have the tools to heal. We either continue to hide our pain or replicate the dysfunctional behaviors we grew up with. Many trauma survivors find themselves stuck in toxic cycles, repeating patterns of self-sacrifice, people-pleasing, or emotional suppression, which leads to emotional exhaustion and burnout.

The trauma of feeling unheard or unimportant in a family system can lead to difficulties in adult relationships. The fear of abandonment, rejection, or being invalidated becomes a constant undercurrent in your interactions. It's hard to let people in when you've been taught, time and time again, that you're not worthy of attention or care. This can contribute to a fear of intimacy, of vulnerability, or even a tendency to push others away before they can get too close.

Steps to Break the Silence

- **Give yourself permission to feel**

    It's okay to be angry, sad, or confused. Your emotions are valid.

    Example: You might find yourself tearing up unexpectedly or feeling irritable for no reason. Instead of pushing it down, pause and say, "It's okay to feel this."

- **Name the trauma**

Identify what you've been through. It's not about reliving the pain but acknowledging it.

Example: Instead of just saying, "I had a tough childhood," you might gently name it: "I experienced emotional neglect," or "I was never made to feel safe."

- **Seek professional help**

  Find a therapist or support group who can walk with you through the healing process.

  Example: You might start by searching online for trauma-informed therapists or asking your doctor for a referral even if you don't feel fully ready to talk yet.

- **Start small**

  It's okay to start by sharing your pain with one person, a trusted friend, or a professional. You don't have to do it all at once.

  Example: You could start by saying, "There's something I've never told anyone, and I don't know where to begin, but I want to try."

The Healing Power of Awareness

For many, the trauma has been stored away in the body, emotions, and subconscious mind for so long that we can hardly recognize it until something triggers it. This could manifest as anxiety, depression, burnout, unhealthy coping mechanisms, or repeating unhealthy patterns in relationships. But when we finally name it, whether it's through self-reflection, speaking with a therapist, or reaching out to a trusted person, we start to take ownership of that piece of our story. It is no longer the thing that runs our lives without our consent.

What Naming Trauma Looks Like in Different Roles:
For Parents:

As a parent, you may feel like you're always "on," responsible for your children's well-being, managing the household, and trying to provide stability for your family. It might be difficult even to remember a time when you had your own emotional needs, much less have the time to address them. The trauma you may have faced growing up, such as neglect, abuse, or witnessing unhealthy relationships, might still play out in the way you parent or interact with your children. You might unconsciously repeat patterns of control, overcompensation, or even emotional unavailability because that's what you learned to survive in your own childhood.

Naming the Trauma: This could involve acknowledging that the way you were raised or the absence of a safe, nurturing environment may be impacting how you parent. Perhaps you've noticed that you're too hard on your children, expecting them to be perfect because you weren't given room to be imperfect. Once you recognize this, you can begin to soften and create a new, healthier environment for your children. You start to see that you are not simply repeating the past; you are choosing how to respond to it now.

For Professionals (Especially High-Achieving Roles):

If you're in a high-pressure role, like a business owner, pastor, or leader, trauma might show up in a very different way. The culture of perfectionism, the constant striving for success, and the need to maintain a "strong" facade can create a resistance to acknowledging past pain. You might think that pushing through and staying focused on external achievements is the only way to prove your worth. But behind that success, you may be carrying years of unaddressed emotional wounds, whether it's burnout from unhealed stress, emotional exhaustion, or a fear of failure that's rooted in childhood trauma or past career setbacks.

Naming the Trauma: In this context, naming trauma might mean realizing that your constant hustle and perfectionism are masking deeper feelings of inadequacy, anxiety, or fear. You may recognize that your overwork is a response to childhood experiences where love and approval were conditional on your achievements. By acknowledging this, you give yourself permission to slow down and let go of the need to always perform at 110%. It allows you to show up as a more authentic, less self-judging version of yourself, one who can both succeed and heal.

For Parents and Caregivers:

Caregivers, especially those working in fields such as nursing, therapy, or education, may find themselves caught in an endless cycle of giving. The silent suffering of caregiving trauma often comes from the emotional labor of being constantly "on" for others, whether it's caring for patients, clients, or loved ones. The emotional exhaustion can be profound, and while you may be constantly nurturing others, you're neglecting your own emotional needs.

Naming the Trauma: For caregivers, naming trauma could mean recognizing that the emotional toll of caring for others, especially without proper self-care, has led to burnout, anxiety, or even physical health issues. You may finally admit that you've been running on empty for too long because you never learned how to prioritize yourself. Once you can name this and acknowledge your own limits, you can begin to set boundaries and ask for help. You stop sacrificing your emotional health for the sake of others and start taking steps to replenish yourself.

For People in Toxic Relationships:

Many people stay silent about the trauma they've endured in relationships, whether that be from abuse, manipulation, or emotional neglect. For those in toxic relationships, naming the trauma can be a painful but necessary first step in breaking free. You might stay in denial about how harmful a relationship is because you fear confrontation, judgment, or rejection. Perhaps you've internalized the messages of your partner, telling yourself that you deserve the treatment you're receiving or that it's not that bad.

Naming the Trauma: This process involves looking honestly at the relationship, acknowledging the damage it's caused, and seeing how it's shaping your present. It's the recognition that you have been subjected to emotional or physical abuse, or that you've been trapped in patterns of codependency. Naming it might be the first time you say, "This is not okay. I am worthy of more than this." By doing this, you can begin to create a plan for safety and healing, whether that's seeking therapy, creating boundaries, or leaving the toxic environment.

For Individuals Who Feel Like They Don't Have a "Voice"

For people who have felt marginalized, whether due to race, gender, socioeconomic status, or any number of reasons, trauma often comes from being silenced or ignored. This is trauma of invisibility, the feeling that your pain, your voice, and your experiences don't matter.

Naming the Trauma: Naming this trauma involves acknowledging that you've been silenced and oppressed, that your feelings have been invalidated or minimized. It means recognizing the power of your voice and the importance of speaking your truth, even when it feels risky or impossible. For some, this is a significant turning point, where the silence is broken, not just for their own healing, but for others who may be feeling the same.

The Journey Toward Healing:

Naming trauma doesn't immediately erase the pain, but it does shift your role from being a passive recipient of hurt to an active participant in your own recovery. Once trauma is named, it can no longer control you from the shadows. You begin to reclaim your power, your narrative, and your future. And while the path to healing is not linear, this first step is critical: you are taking back control over your life.

Now, gently ask yourself, what moments, big or small, may have shaped your behaviors or the way you see yourself today? Have you noticed patterns that seem to repeat in your life, even though you've tried to move on? What might be the underlying source of these patterns? Acknowledge the feelings that come up, this is the first step in turning the page to a new chapter of healing.

Key Insights from Chapter 6

Chapter 6 explores the unseen forces of trauma and how they quietly shape our lives, often without our awareness. Many of us carry emotional weight, stress, and tension without identifying the root cause, and recognizing how trauma influences us subconsciously is the first step toward healing. Strength, it shows, can often be a mask; pushing through, surviving, and keeping everything together can hide the pain we silently bear.

True healing begins when we acknowledge that pain and allow ourselves the space to recover. Awareness is a powerful tool in this process; by recognizing and naming trauma, we reclaim control of our narrative and move from mere survival to genuine repair. Trauma is not just a single event but an ongoing process that shapes our behaviors, beliefs, and even our life choices, often remaining unnoticed until a breaking point prompts change.

Yet, we are never truly alone in this journey. Recognizing trauma in others fosters empathy, understanding, and meaningful connection. Ultimately, healing requires vulnerability allowing ourselves to be seen, to let down our guard, and to trust others is essential for transformation. It is through this openness, despite the fear of judgment, that true resilience and growth emerge.

Restorative Reflection

Have you ever experienced a moment when you realized something was affecting your life much more deeply than you had understood at first?

_____

_____

_____

How did that realization shift the way you saw your own struggles, and what steps did you take afterward to address it?

_____

_____

_____

Section 3

Strengthening

Building a life of boundaries, resilience, and compassion

CHAPTER 7

Resilience in the Blueprint: Designing a Future Built on Strength

When life breaks you down, resilience helps you rebuild higher.

When life breaks you down, resilience is the quiet force that helps you rebuild. But rebuilding isn't about rushing back to who you were before the storm. It's about constructing something new, something more substantial, sometimes something you didn't expect to become.

I remember a time when everything in my life seemed to fall apart all at once. It wasn't a single disaster but a slow unraveling: relationships that frayed, dreams that felt out of reach, a constant weight pressing on my chest. I thought resilience meant "bouncing back" quickly, being strong enough to ignore the pain, to hide the cracks so no one could see. But that wasn't a real strength. It was exhaustion masked as bravery.

True resilience, I've come to understand, is something deeper and quieter. It's the courage to face the broken pieces of your life honestly, to stop running, and to start piecing them back together with patience and care. It's the willingness to say, "These hurts, but I will not let it defeat me."

Many people say, "Kids are so resilient." And it's true, children often survive unimaginable hardships. Trauma, loss, neglect. They adapt in ways that keep them alive. But surviving isn't the same as healing. Those early wounds, if left unaddressed, become silent architects of our adult struggles. They shape how we trust, how we love, and how we believe in ourselves.

The resilience we develop in childhood is often survival-mode resilience. It's not the same as choosing to heal as an adult. Childhood resilience might keep us afloat, but it doesn't erase the scars beneath the surface. Sometimes those scars feel like invisible weights, dragging us down even when everything looks fine on the outside.

Resilience isn't about pretending the pain isn't there or pushing through without pause. It's about walking with the pain, learning its contours, understanding its roots, and deciding day by day how to move forward in spite of it.

There were nights when I laid awake, overwhelmed by grief and doubt, wondering if I could carry this burden any longer. It wasn't just physical tiredness; it was a deep soul fatigue. But slowly, through the quiet moments of surrender, I found a new kind of strength. Not the strength of never breaking, but the strength of rising even when broken.

Resilience is not a race. It's not a competition to see who can be the "strongest." It's a long, winding path that winds through uncertainty and fear, marked by moments of doubt and sudden breakthroughs.

I remember a moment standing in the ruins of what I thought my life would be. I felt lost, fragile, and scared. But I also felt a flicker of something else. A tiny spark of hope, that maybe, just maybe, this wasn't the end. Maybe there was something still waiting to be built from the ashes.

That's what resilience is: the faith to believe that your story isn't over, even when you can't see the ending. It's the courage to write each day's following line, even if it's shaky or uncertain.

My mentor, Crystal, often reminded me, "It's not how you start, it's how you finish." That wisdom stayed with me. It meant that, no matter the brokenness, mistakes, or detours, the final chapters can still be beautiful, full of growth, healing, and new beginnings.

So, resilience isn't about being unbreakable. It's about embracing your brokenness and deciding what kind of life you will build from it. It's about becoming the architect of your own healing, designing a blueprint that holds space for pain, hope, and transformation.

The Power in Every Moment of Suffering

Reflecting on my journey, I believe God wastes nothing. Our struggles don't happen by accident or without purpose. There's meaning in every hardship, even when it's hard to see. Sometimes, when caught in the thick of pain, it feels like life is simply handing us chaos for no reason. But looking back, I realize that every challenge was like a thread woven into a larger tapestry, a story that's uniquely mine and crafted with intention.

Pain, heartbreak, and disappointment aren't meaningless. God uses every challenge to shape us and prepare us for what's next. These moments of suffering aren't failures; they're part of a divine process leading to growth and transformation. They are not wasted. Even the darkest moments serve as silent teachers, revealing strengths we never knew we had, forcing us to pause, re-evaluate, and grow beyond our previous limits.

In the silence of suffering, it's easy to feel lost, as if pain defines you. You might feel stuck, invisible, and disconnected, even though you're doing everything "right," yet still feel unseen. That's one of the hardest parts of living with a pain that isolates you, makes you question your worth, and blurs the lines between your true self and the wounds you carry. You may wonder if this loneliness will ever end or if it will be a permanent shadow in your life.

But over time, I shifted my view. Suffering, though isolating and painful, can bring a deeper understanding of yourself and the world. It invites you to slow down, to listen more carefully to what your heart is saying beneath the noise. You begin to see that your pain is a passage, a threshold that, when crossed, reveals new landscapes of empathy, resilience, and purpose.

It's not about bouncing back to who you were before; it's about finding meaning and strength in the struggle and trusting that this struggle is a bridge to something greater. Healing is not a rewind button; it's an evolution. You become someone who can hold both the pain and the hope simultaneously, realizing they coexist and feed your growth.

You might question if you're strong enough to carry this weight. It's a quiet burden, carried alone, feeling like no one understands. You may fear that speaking up will make others uncomfortable or see you differently. That fear can be paralyzing. Yet, it's important to remember that vulnerability is not a weakness; it's a doorway to connection and healing. When you dare to share your truth, you often find unexpected allies who carry you in ways you never imagined.

Even in the silence, unseen battles are being fought with courage and dignity. Don't be ashamed of your struggle. Some of the most brutal battles are fought silently, unseen, but no less real or valuable. The world may not always witness your fight, but that doesn't make it any less heroic. Your courage in the quiet is profound.

This uncomfortable space is powerful. Its transformation is in progress. Growth often feels messy and uncertain, but these are the places where new foundations are laid, foundations built on authenticity, courage, and self-awareness.

Even if the world doesn't hear your pain, it's meaningful. Your resilience builds quietly, preparing you for the strength ahead. Like roots growing deep beneath the surface, your inner strength is forming, anchoring you for whatever comes next.

In this silence, you learn to let go of unrealistic expectations. You forgive yourself for not being perfect, for not pleasing everyone, for not having it all together. This forgiveness is a revolutionary act, a release from chains that have kept you striving for approval instead of peace.

And in that forgiveness, you find a deeper resilience a grounded strength that accepts your humanity and imperfections. You come to understand that perfection was never the goal; it's your authenticity and perseverance that genuinely matter.

Through every struggle, you become stronger, wiser, and better prepared for what's ahead. These experiences are not setbacks but steppingstones, each one equipping you with insight and compassion.

Your silence does not define you. You are defined by your ability to endure, to shift expectations, and rise above pressures that once suffocated you. The quiet strength within you speaks louder than any external noise.

Say it with me: It's okay not to be perfect. It's OK not to meet everyone's expectations. Your worth isn't tied to pleasing others or always being "fine." It's tied to your ability to keep going, growing, and emerging stronger from the silence.

In the quiet moments when no one is watching, when the noise of the world fades away, that's where true strength is forged. It's in those silent battles, the ones that leave no visible scars, that your resilience takes root. You don't have to shout your victories or explain your pain. Your journey is yours alone, and every step forward, even the smallest, is a testament to your courage.

Remember, healing isn't a race or a checklist. It's a winding path with twists, turns, and unexpected pauses. Sometimes, the bravest thing you can do is simply to keep showing up for yourself, day after day, even when it feels like you're standing still. That perseverance, that quiet insistence on moving forward, is the real measure of your worth.

So, embrace the silence. Let it be a place where you nurture hope, rebuild trust in yourself, and find the courage to rewrite your story on your terms. Because you are not defined by the pain you've endured, but by the strength you've cultivated in its aftermath.

The Resilience Toolbox: Cultivating Strength in Adversity

Life doesn't hand us a perfect blueprint. Sometimes, the design cracks under pressure.

You might feel lost in a storm with no exit, maybe you're a parent holding it together, a leader carrying burdens, or someone always expected to have it all together.

You wonder if resilience is something others have, but not you.

Maybe you doubt if you can get back up.

Here's what I've learned: resilience isn't innate. It's a toolbox you build over time. Sometimes through pain, sometimes through stubbornness.

And even now, in the mess of your struggle, you're building it.

Resilience isn't about skipping the hard parts or pretending all is fine.

It's about navigating the mess and emerging stronger on the other side.

That's the real work. And it looks different for everyone.

This chapter shares tools I've found helpful that you can start using now to rebuild and reinforce your blueprint of resilience.

1. Acceptance: Stop Fighting the Blueprint

When everything feels like it's falling apart, your instinct is to fight, push away pain, or deny the cracks.

But imagine trying to fix a building while ignoring fractures in its foundation. The damage worsens when it's unseen.

Acceptance isn't surrender or saying, "this is okay."

It's facing reality, no matter how scary or uncomfortable.

I tell my clients the first step is brutal honesty.

Where are you really? What's beneath the surface?

It's easy to hide behind distractions, but to rebuild, you must see the cracks even if it hurts.

Acceptance means saying, "This is hard. I'm struggling. I'm not okay." Without shame or judgment.

Think of acceptance as opening the blueprint to find damage.

You can't fix what you don't see.

Admitting cracks creates space for real work.

You permit yourself to be vulnerable, and vulnerability brings strength.

This step is uncomfortable because it forces you to stop running or fighting what's inside.

However, without acceptance, you merely patch problems without addressing the root cause.

When you accept your pain, you take ownership of your healing.

You become the architect of your recovery.

From here, you choose what to repair, reinforce, or let go.

Remember: acceptance isn't the final goal; it's the foundation for what comes next.

2. Self-Compassion: Be the Builder, Not the Critic

We sabotage ourselves, expecting perfection.

When things fall apart, the inner critic shouts, "You're weak. You're failing."

What if you treated yourself like a builder fixing a broken house, not a judge condemning a failed project?

You deserve patience and kindness.

Struggling doesn't mean you're beyond repair; it means you're in the middle of the process.

3. Perspective: See the Blueprint, Not Just the Rubble

In crisis, it's hard to see past the wreckage the pain, the chaos, the collapse all blurs your vision.

But your story isn't defined by this moment or season.

Try zooming out.

Step back from the rubble and see the whole blueprint: the foundation, the cracks, and the future you want to build.

Right now, isn't the finished product.

It's a draft, a rough sketch, messy and incomplete.

It might feel flawed beyond repair.

But what if this stage of challenges, setbacks, and pain add something valuable to your blueprint?

Sometimes cracks aren't just damage, they're openings.

Openings for insights, strengths, directions you never imagined.

Ask yourself:

What is this experience teaching me?

How might this struggle shape a stronger, wiser me?

What parts of my blueprint am I invited to redesign, rebuild, or reinforce?

Seeing your situation this way doesn't minimize pain.

It lets you acknowledge where you are without being consumed by it.

It reminds you that even broken parts can become essential pieces of your future.

Perspective isn't denial, it's recognizing the blueprint beneath the rubble and trusting reconstruction.

The path forward may be unclear, but the design is unfolding.

And you are still the architect.

4. Support: Find Your Crew

No builder works alone.

Whether building a home, designing a plan, or rebuilding life, you need others.

People who lend tools, share advice, or steady you when the work gets heavy.

Reaching out might feel like a failure or weakness, but it's actually a smart and practical move.

It's not falling apart; it's a commitment to rebuild, no matter how hard.

Your crew could be friends, family, mentors, or communities.

People who listen without judgment, remind you of your worth, and help carry your weight when you feel weak.

I tell clients this is the most important part of rebuilding.

Surround yourself with those who genuinely support and understand your journey.

Your blueprint isn't just yours; it's stronger with others.

Support might be a text, a coffee, or a silent moment.

Or advice, encouragement, or a helping hand.

Don't wait until you're overwhelmed to reach out.

Build your crew now so they catch you before you fall.

I laugh now because my mentor always knew when something was wrong.

No matter how much I said, "I'm fine," she'd ask, "What's wrong?"

I was the master of silent suffering but having someone who saw through that made all the difference.

That connection is a lifeline when rebuilding.

You're not alone.

5. Purpose: Anchor Your Design

Purpose isn't just about others.

It starts with yourself.

When life feels unstable, purpose is the anchor that helps you stand firm.

It's the quiet commitment to keep building even when it feels impossible.

Purpose doesn't need to be grand.

It may be as simple as choosing to care for yourself or create space for peace.

It's what you need to feel whole, not what others expect.

Purpose might mean setting boundaries to protect your energy.

Carving minutes to breathe or reflect.

Saying no to what drains you.

Saying yes to what feeds your soul.

These small acts are resilience in action.

Proof you prioritize yourself and your healing.

Purpose grounds you in truth and fuels your strength, one step at a time.

Resilience is a Work in Progress

Right now, you may feel like you're barely holding on.

But every step facing pain, asking for help, and reminding yourself why you go on, adds strength to your structure.

This toolbox is yours. Use it.

It won't erase cracks overnight but helps build something real and lasting.

Your story isn't over. It's being rewritten.

Rising after struggle doesn't mean pain disappears.

It doesn't erase defeat, failure, or exhaustion.

It means choosing to keep moving forward even when you want to stop.

This choice is often the hardest, especially when silent suffering weighs heavily and the path seems unclear.

Resilience isn't grand drama.

It's found in quiet, consistent choices to show up for yourself even when exhausted, overwhelmed, or uncertain.

It's the small victories: courage to face a new day, strength to ask for help, grace to forgive your imperfections.

True resilience lives in these simple acts of persistence, especially when the future is unclear.

Rising looks different for everyone.

Sometimes it's permission to rest and recharge.

Other times it's setting boundaries, saying no to drains, and challenging negative thoughts.

Or reaching out when you've always handled things alone.

Or deciding to stop letting your inner critic define your worth.

The one constant?

Resilience isn't bouncing back perfectly.

It's progress.

Rising even if it's slow, messy, and painful.

Each rise builds strength.

Each act sends a message:

Keep going. Even when hard. Even when impossible. Just keep moving forward.

Key Insights from Chapter 7

Chapter 7 explores resilience not as a fixed destination but as an ongoing journey. It involves learning to rise each day after being broken, not by avoiding pain, but by facing it directly. While unhealed wounds influence us, they do not define our identity. The pain we carry often shows up in our relationships, decisions, and self-view, and real growth happens only when we confront that pain honestly. Suffering holds both purpose and potential, as every challenge, no matter how painful, contributes to shaping and preparing us for the future. Acceptance is the foundation of healing; when we recognize our struggles without denial or shame, we allow genuine repair and rebuilding to begin.

The chapter emphasizes the importance of self-compassion over self-criticism, encouraging us to treat ourselves like patient builders working through a process rather than harsh judges demanding perfection. Perspective plays a transformative role by helping us see beyond immediate pain and chaos to the broader "blueprint" of our lives, revealing growth opportunities we might otherwise overlook. Support systems are essential for making the rebuilding process stronger and more sustainable, especially when we surround ourselves with people who listen, encourage, and share the load. Purpose acts as an anchor for resilience, with small, daily acts of self-care, such as setting boundaries and prioritizing well-being, fueling the strength needed to keep moving forward.

Finally, resilience is shown to look different for everyone. It often manifests in quiet, consistent acts of persistence rather than dramatic moments. To rise means to keep moving forward despite pain. True resilience is the choice to continue even when the path is messy, slow, or painful.

Restorative Reflection

When have you chosen to keep going, even when it felt impossible?

_____

_____

_____

Which of the resilience tools, acceptance, self-compassion, perspective, support, or purpose, do you feel you need most right now?

_____

_____

_____

How might reaching out for support change the way you navigate your struggles?

_____

_____

_____

CHAPTER 8

Constructing Boundaries: Protecting Your Emotional Space

Sometimes the strongest people are the quietest sufferers, holding together a world that no one sees is unraveling.

When You're the One Who Holds It All

I've seen it in pastors, parents, business owners, high-achieving professionals, ministry leaders, caregivers, therapists, and in my own reflection. These are the people who are the rock, the sounding board, the dependable ones. The ones everyone calls in a crisis.

In architecture, boundaries define a space separating the inside from the outside. In our emotional lives, boundaries serve the same purpose. They tell others where we begin and end. Without them, our emotional space becomes overrun, not because others mean harm, but because we haven't clearly laid out the limits.

Many of us were never taught how to build healthy emotional boundaries. Instead, we were taught to be available, to be "nice," never to disappoint. Somewhere along the way, we learned that saying no meant being selfish or unkind.

But here's the truth: every strong structure needs clear lines. A foundation cracks when it bears too much weight for an extended period. The same is true for you.

Setting boundaries is not shutting people out. It's about designing a space where genuine connection can occur without resentment, burnout, or self-betrayal. It's a declaration that your emotional safety matters.

Start small. Maybe it's not answering emails after a particular hour, or saying, "I can't take this on right now" without explaining yourself. Boundaries aren't walls; they're blueprints for safe connection.

The Hidden Weight of Being "Okay"

There were seasons when I showed up for clients by day and family by night, then collapsed, feeling hollow inside. People called me strong, unaware that my strength was a result of being in a state of survival. I wasn't thriving; I was unraveling silently.

Being "okay" can become a role, especially when vulnerability feels unsafe or asking for help seems like a burden. Many of us have learned to equate independence with worthiness, believing that needing help makes us too much.

But humans were never designed to heal alone.

Finding a Community That Actually Uplifts You

I often ask clients: "Do the people around you know how to support you?"

The silence that follows is telling. Many have networks but not a community. They're surrounded but unseen. The history of being let down keeps walls up and needs unspoken.

But even the strongest need support. Finding it starts with clarity and intention, not just proximity.

Engage in spaces that light you up, not drain you. Creative classes, yoga, running clubs, faith gatherings, advocacy groups, wherever you can be you, not just your role.

"These aren't hobbies; they are access points to belonging."

Shared interests lead to shared values, where real connection begins.

Say What You Need Out Loud

People aren't mind readers.

We assume they "just know" how to support us. But they don't, not because they don't care, but because we never showed them how.

Saying, "I don't need advice right now, just presence," or "It would help to know you're praying for me," is a powerful act of self-respect.

Being clear isn't a weakness. It's wisdom. It allows others to love you well. And if they can't? That's information about their limits, not a rejection of you.

Online Doesn't Mean Less Real

Community often starts online.

I've seen deep relationships form in virtual groups, support spaces, and mentorship communities. For many, these spaces become lifelines, especially during illness, caregiving, or trauma.

Face-to-face connection is vital, but don't underestimate the power of a curated online community. Sometimes it's what keeps you afloat until in-person connection returns.

Start Small, But Be Consistent

Community isn't always big groups gathering weekly. For many adults, it's quieter, and that's okay.

Start with one or two people. Check in regularly. Invite depth. Show up when it matters.

"It's not about quantity; it's about quality and consistency. Water what waters you."

Meaningful relationships often begin with casual texts, quick coffee, shared tasks, and deepen through showing up for each other in the mess.

Healing Happens in Reciprocity

Healing often comes not just from receiving help, but also from helping others.

Being seen as needed even when broken reconnects you to your own strength. Volunteering, mentoring, or simply showing up for a friend can restore your humanity.

"We don't heal in isolation. We heal in mutual exchange of care and presence."

Don't Give Up After One Try

Many get stuck after one bad experience. A group that feels off, a friend who dismisses, an effort that falls flat.

Then they quit.

But connection takes time. Trial and error. Courage. Letting yourself be seen again and again.

You won't be everyone's cup of tea. Not every space will feel safe. But your people exist.

Every attempt, even painful ones, brings you closer to what fits.

Sometimes, the most important thing is to show up one more time.

You Deserve to Be Held, Too

Let me say it plainly:

You are not too much.

You are not a burden.

You are not the exception to belonging.

You deserve support. You deserve rest. You deserve a community that sees your whole self, not just the parts that are easy or useful.

It may take time to find that community, but you are worth that time.

Key Insights from Chapter 8

Chapter 8 highlights the crucial role emotional boundaries play in protecting our mental and emotional well-being. Just as architectural blueprints define the structure and limits of a building, boundaries help define personal space and prevent burnout and resentment. The chapter also challenges the misconception that strength means being invulnerable. Many people who appear strong are actually silently suffering, masking their struggles behind a facade of being "okay." Vulnerability, in contrast, is essential for healing and forming authentic connections, as it allows others to understand and support us.

The chapter emphasizes that true community is about the quality of relationships, not the quantity. Consistent and meaningful connections foster a sense of belonging more than large social networks or superficial relationships. Effective communication is another key theme, expressing your needs clearly is an act of self-respect and a necessary step to receive proper support. The chapter also recognizes the value of online communities, which can offer genuine connection and support, especially when face-to-face options are limited.

Healing is depicted as a reciprocal process; by supporting others, we can also restore our own strength and purpose. Persistence is vital in finding and building a safe emotional community, and setbacks should not discourage this journey. Finally, the chapter reassures readers that they deserve to be held and supported fully. No one is "too much" or a burden; every person's whole self deserves rest, care, and belonging.

Restorative Reflection

Where in your life do you feel most emotionally "crowded" or overextended?

_____

_____

_____

What might that be telling you about boundaries that need reinforcing?

_____

_____

_____

What does a healthy emotional boundary look like for you right now?

_____

_____

_____

Describe it as if you were drafting it into a blueprint. What's included? What's not?

_____

_____

_____

How have your silent struggles shaped the way you approach boundaries today?

_____

_____

_____

Are you more guarded, more open, or somewhere in between?

_____

_____

_____

Who in your life consistently respects your boundaries, and who doesn't?

_____

_____

_____

How can you respond differently in each relationship?

_____

_____

_____

What's one small boundary you can begin to practice this week?

_____

_____

_____

(Think of this as laying the first brick, not building the whole structure at once.)

_____

_____

_____

CHAPTER 9

The Invisible Weight of Expectations and the Power of Self-Compassion

Behind every silent sufferer is an invisible weight, a complex web of expectations woven by the world, by those we love, and sometimes by ourselves.

Expectations don't announce themselves with fanfare; instead, they settle quietly, pressing down until it feels impossible to breathe.

For many, the unspoken rule is to be strong at all times, to carry burdens without complaint, and to present a version of "fine" that masks the turmoil underneath. This relentless pressure fuels a cycle of perfectionism and burnout, leaving silent sufferers exhausted, isolated, and questioning their worth.

But what if breaking free doesn't mean meeting those expectations better, but learning to meet yourself with kindness instead?

Self-Compassion as a Radical Act

Self-compassion is not just a buzzword. It's a radical act of resistance against the shame and exhaustion that come from trying to be everything to everyone. When you show yourself kindness and let go of perfectionism, you disrupt the cycle of self-criticism and guilt.

It's about allowing yourself to be imperfect, vulnerable, and human, and in that, finding true strength. The world may not always offer you the space to fail, to rest, or not to have it all together, but you can choose to create that space for yourself.

By practicing self-compassion, you honor your humanity and recognize that you don't have to do it all or be perfect to be worthy. In fact, it's your imperfections that make you real, and embracing them is what finally enables you to break the silence of self-doubt.

The Common Misconception About Strength

In a world that values self-sufficiency and composure, strength is often mistaken for stoicism. We've been conditioned to believe that being strong means keeping our emotions in check, staying unfazed under pressure, and never letting anyone see our weaknesses. It's the image of the person who carries the weight of the world on their shoulders, without ever showing a sign of strain. But this is a limited, one-dimensional view of what it means to be strong.

The Hidden Cost of Perfection

For many people, especially those in leadership or caregiving roles, there's an unspoken expectation to be "perfect," or at least to appear perfect. The fear of being seen as anything less than composed, particularly when others depend on you, can lead to self-neglect, emotional exhaustion, and burnout. But this idea that strength means perfection comes at a high cost: the loss of vulnerability, honesty, and connection. It isolates us from others, making us feel as though we must carry every burden alone.

Real Strength is About Honesty

Real strength is not about masking your struggles or trying to live up to an unattainable standard. True strength lies in the ability to be honest with yourself and others, even when it feels uncomfortable. It takes immense courage to acknowledge that you are struggling, to admit that you are not invincible, and to recognize that it's okay to ask for help. This kind of honesty isn't weakness; it's radical authenticity. It's the ability to look at your situation and say, "This is hard, and I need support." That kind of strength is often unseen, but it allows us to build something sustainable and lasting, both in ourselves and in our relationships.

Strength Is in the Acknowledgment of Limits

True strength lies in knowing your limits and respecting them. It's the ability to say "I can't do it all" without feeling like you're letting anyone down. In fact, acknowledging your limits rather than pretending you have none makes you stronger, as it demonstrates that you understand your own needs. It's like a house with a solid foundation: it's not the walls that hold everything up, but the strong base that ensures the entire structure can stand tall. By knowing when to stop, rest, or ask for help, you ensure that you won't crumble under the weight of expectations.

As a therapist and in My Personal Life

As much as I guide others through the labyrinth of their struggles, I've had to walk through it myself. There are moments, too many to count, where I forget the very lessons, I teach. I forget that I, too, deserve to be heard. There was a time when I didn't feel I could share the weight I carried with anyone. I feared judgment, felt inadequate, or assumed that asking for help would somehow make me weak.

It's easy to believe that, as someone who helps others, I should always have it together. But the truth is, I am human. And just like my clients, I'm on this journey of healing, learning, and growing. The work I do with others is not separate from my own life. It's a continual process, a rhythm of teaching and being taught, of holding space for others while also needing that space held for me.

This disconnect, this silent assumption that I needed to be "fine," slowly led me to burnout. It wasn't sudden. It was like that slow simmer we talked about earlier, the kind that builds over time without a clear, immediate warning. Eventually, one day, it all became too much. I walked away from my job. I quit, exhausted and broken, because I had forgotten to apply the very principles I was preaching. I had ignored my own need for vulnerability and connection, thinking that if I didn't have it all together, I wasn't "good enough" to help others.

But what I've learned is that vulnerability is not a weakness. In fact, it's the bridge to healing. It's the doorway to authenticity. And when I returned to the principles, I teach my clients, naming the pain, embracing vulnerability, seeking connection, I began to heal, not in a neat, linear way, but in a messy, beautiful, human way. I'm still healing.

This journey of my personal healing and my professional life is intertwined. Every client I help, every lesson I teach, is a reminder that I, too, am a work in progress. And that's okay. It's in the messy, ongoing work that we discover our most actual strength.

The Strength in Vulnerability

Vulnerability has often been mischaracterized as weakness, especially for those who are used to being seen as the strong ones. But vulnerability is actually one of the most courageous acts a person can perform. It means exposing parts of yourself that feel raw or uncomfortable, whether it's admitting you're struggling emotionally or showing that you don't have all the answers. Vulnerability is the willingness to be real, even when it feels risky or uncertain. It is through vulnerability that we find authentic connections with others and create a sense of mutual understanding and support.

Naming Your Struggle as an Act of Resilience

Naming your struggle, whether it's anxiety, loss, exhaustion, or doubt, is not a sign of failure, but an act of resilience. It's the first step in facing the challenge head-on, without letting it define you. When you give your pain a name, you begin to reclaim control. You stop being at the mercy of an unnamed, overwhelming feeling and start to engage with it directly. You start to see it as something you can work through, not something that will swallow you whole. Naming it gives you the power to face it, understand it, and ultimately move beyond it.

Rewriting the Narrative of Strength

There is an unspoken narrative in society that strength equals never breaking, never faltering, and never showing vulnerability. But the truth is, the strongest people are often the ones who have allowed themselves to break and then rebuild, who have shown up with scars and all, and who have let themselves be human. Strength is not about hiding your cracks; it's about embracing them, learning from them, and finding the courage to rise again. When you redefine strength this way, you open yourself up to a whole new world of possibilities. You start to see that real strength lies not in perfection, but in the ability to persist and grow, even when the journey isn't easy.

Silence vs. Solitude

There's a difference between being silent and being alone. Solitude can be healing, a place to reflect and gather strength. But silence that isolates and hides pain can be harmful. Learning to distinguish between the two helps you honor your need for peace while still seeking connection and support.

Your Voice Matters

Your story, your pain, your struggle, no matter how quiet or hidden, matters. When you break the silence, you reclaim your power. You remind yourself and the world that your experience is valid and worthy of care. Speaking your truth is a form of resistance against invisibility and denial.

The Power of Being Seen and Heard

Healing doesn't require a perfect audience or an immediate solution. It begins with being seen and heard. It's simple, but profoundly transformative. When someone listens to your struggles without judgment, without rushing in to offer advice or fix things, you begin to release the heavy burden of isolation. You start to feel less alone. And in that space of connection, healing has room to grow.

This is why we often hear that the most powerful thing you can do for someone going through a hard time is to just be there, to listen without the need to "do" anything. In those moments of deep pain or confusion, the most significant step forward is not to have all the answers, but to let someone share their heart without fear of being dismissed or minimized.

The Challenge of Being Heard in High-Pressure Roles

For some, especially those in positions of responsibility or authority, allowing yourself to be vulnerable, to be truly seen and heard, feels nearly impossible. These are people who've been conditioned to be the strong ones, the ones who hold it all together. They might be leaders, caregivers, or providers, and their emotional needs are often sidelined because of the expectations others have placed on them.

- **Pastors:** Pastors are expected to provide spiritual guidance and emotional support to others while remaining composed and unwavering. The idea of a pastor struggling or feeling lost can be difficult to reconcile with the public image of someone who is a constant source of strength. But the truth is, pastors face personal struggles, doubts, and exhaustion too, often in silence. They're asked to hold space for others' grief without being given space for their own.

- **Business** Owners and Executives: Entrepreneurs and professionals are often seen as the driving force behind their companies, expected to lead with confidence, strategic vision, and relentless drive. Yet, the emotional toll of decision-making, long hours, and isolation can be overwhelming. In the competitive world of business, showing vulnerability can feel like a weakness, especially when their success is tied to their ability to always appear strong.

- **Parents and Caregivers:** Parents, especially those who are caregivers for children with special needs or aging parents, are often expected to be the unshakeable foundation of the family. They give so much to others, but when it comes to expressing their own struggles, there is often a sense of guilt or shame. They might feel that they should be strong for their children, not showing them the human side of their struggles. This can make it difficult to ask for help, let alone express their pain or frustration.

- **Therapists and Counselors:** It can be a profound struggle for therapists to admit when they are struggling. They're expected to have all the answers, to be the one who listens and guides others through their pain. But therapists are human too. The emotional toll of hearing others' struggles, coupled with their own personal challenges, can feel like an unbearable weight, and the constant "giving" can lead to burnout and exhaustion.

- **Healthcare Workers:** Doctors, nurses, and other medical professionals are often hailed as heroes for their tireless work, especially in times of crisis. But they, too, are human, facing their own fears, stress, and emotional fatigue. The long hours, trauma, and moral injury from seeing suffering daily can lead to compassion fatigue. However, in an environment where strength and professionalism are highly valued, there's little room for them to express their vulnerability without fearing they'll be seen as unfit for their role.

- **Teachers and Educators:** Teachers are expected to be nurturing, patient, and emotionally available for their students. Yet, many teachers carry the weight of emotional burnout, financial strain, and personal life challenges while showing up every day for their students. The pressure to constantly be "on" can make it difficult for them to admit when they are struggling, as they fear it may undermine their authority or professionalism.

Therapist's Perspective: The Importance of Being Heard

Healing begins with being heard. In my work as a therapist, one of the most profound shifts I see in my clients is when they finally allow themselves to be seen. They often enter therapy thinking that they need to have everything figured out, that they need to present the "best version" of themselves. But the real breakthrough happens when they realize that the healing process is about being honest and vulnerable, not perfect.

Healing doesn't require a perfect audience or immediate solutions. It begins simply by being seen and heard. When someone listens without judgment, your pain loses some of its power to isolate you. You begin to feel connected, less alone, and more ready to face the next step on your journey. As a therapist, I witness this every day.

One of the most profound things that I can do for my clients is to simply listen. To listen without judgment. To offer empathy, not solutions. And in doing so, I provide them with the space they need to process their pain and, eventually, begin to heal.

But you don't need to be in therapy to be heard. You can create this space in your life, too. You can reach out to trusted friends, family, or even a support group. The key is to find people who are willing to sit with you in your pain, without trying to fix it or make it go away. True healing happens when we allow ourselves to be heard, not fixed.

The Need for Compassionate Presence

Simply asking, "What do you need from me right now?" can be a revelation to someone who has spent so long not knowing how to ask for what they need. When someone responds with care, "I'm here for you," it might be the first time that person has felt truly seen in a long time. It's an invitation to lean into the vulnerability of being human, and an acknowledgment that it's okay to not have all the answers, to not always be okay.

You can't heal in silence. Healing is a process of being seen, being heard, and being cared for. And that starts with finding the courage to name your struggle, no matter how difficult it may be.

Remember: You Are Not Alone

Now, allow yourself to be honest in your response. It's okay if the answers don't come right away. Healing doesn't rush, and neither should you.

It's easy to believe that the weight you carry is yours alone, that the pain you feel is too much for others to understand. But that's far from the truth. Countless others around you, often quietly, are bearing their own burdens. We all carry silent struggles that we may not speak about, yet they shape us just the same.

When I reflect on my own journey, how I've learned, stumbled, and relearned the value of connection, I realize how critical it is to create and find a community where silence is understood, and where voices can be nurtured without fear of judgment. In breaking your own silence, you permit others to do the same. It's not about sharing every detail, but simply creating a space where vulnerability is welcomed and healing is nurtured.

In this shared space, where people truly listen and connect, a chorus of healing begins. It's not just about you finding support; it's about building a collective strength, one that allows each of us to rise from our silent struggles together. The more we speak, the more we invite others to speak. The more we heal, the more we can help others heal.

Healing doesn't always happen in grand gestures; sometimes it's in the quiet, consistent presence of someone who understands that pain is not a weakness, but a human experience that binds us. So don't be afraid to reach out and share your voice. In doing so, you'll help create a ripple of connection, understanding, and hope for yourself and those around you. You are never truly alone.

Key Insights from Chapter 9

Chapter 9 explores the invisible weight of expectations that many silent sufferers carry daily. These expectations come from society, loved ones, and even from within us, creating a heavy pressure to always be strong and composed. This invisible burden often leads to exhaustion, isolation, and a deep questioning of self-worth. The chapter highlights that the path to healing isn't about meeting these expectations perfectly but about meeting ourselves with kindness and self-compassion.

Self-compassion is presented as a radical and transformative act. It challenges the common cycle of perfectionism, self-criticism, and guilt by encouraging us to embrace our imperfections and vulnerabilities. True strength, the chapter argues, is not about masking struggles or pretending to have everything together. Instead, it lies in the courage to be honest about our difficulties and to ask for support when needed. Recognizing and respecting our limits is essential; acknowledging that we cannot do it all is a sign of wisdom and resilience rather than failure.

Vulnerability, often misunderstood as weakness, is reframed as a powerful tool for connection and healing. When we allow ourselves to be vulnerable, we open the door to authentic relation-ships and mutual understanding. Naming our struggles, whether anxiety, burnout, or doubt, is not a sign of defeat but an act of resilience that helps us regain control over our pain and begin the healing process.

A central message of the chapter is the critical importance of being heard. Healing starts when someone listens without judgment or the urge to fix things. This compassionate presence creates space for us to share our pain safely, reducing the isolation that silent suffering often brings. The chapter also acknowledges the challenges faced by people in high-pressure roles, such as leaders, caregivers, and therapists, who may find it especially difficult to show vulnerability but need it the most.

Ultimately, Chapter 9 encourages breaking the silence by creating spaces where vulnerability is welcomed and healing is nurtured. It reminds us that we are not alone in our struggles and that sharing our stories can foster a collective strength that benefits both ourselves and others. Healing is an ongoing journey that requires honesty, connection, and self-compassion.

Restorative Reflection

How often have I felt the pressure to be "strong" by hiding my struggles?

_____

_____

_____

What would it feel like to name my pain out loud, even just to myself?

_____

_____

_____

Who in my life would I trust to hear me without judgment?

_____

_____

_____

What would healing look like for me if it started with simply being seen and heard?

_____

_____

_____

Technology and Trauma: The Digital Paradox

In today's hyper-connected world, technology serves as both a bridge and a barrier. It allows us to stay connected, find support, and access resources, yet it can also deepen our isolation and prolong our pain. For those who are already carrying trauma, the pressures of constant availability and the demands of the digital world can exacerbate stress, leaving little room for healing. The very tools meant to help us connect and heal can, in fact, sometimes prevent us from truly confronting our struggles. This section examines the multifaceted role that technology plays in both hindering and facilitating trauma recovery, and how we can strike a balance in an ever-evolving world.

Technology as a Double-Edged Sword

Connection vs. Isolation: Technology has revolutionized the way we connect, enabling us to reach out across the world with a single click. But for those suffering silently, this connection often feels shallow and isolating. The curated "perfect lives" we see on social media can deepen feelings of inadequacy, comparison, and self-doubt. It exacerbates the trauma for many who feel like they don't measure up. At the same time, digital communities, including virtual therapy, have also become vital lifelines. These online spaces provide a safe, sometimes anonymous platform for individuals to share their struggles and initiate the healing process. They help bridge the gap between isolation and connection, providing people with the support they may not yet feel ready to seek in person.

Escaping vs. Facing: In today's world, escaping pain through technology is easier than ever. Whether it's binge-watching a show, scrolling mindlessly through social media, or getting lost in virtual worlds, the distractions are endless. These distractions can offer temporary relief, but they also prevent us from addressing our pain head-on. The longer we avoid facing our trauma, the more it embeds itself in our lives, and the harder it becomes to heal. Technology, while providing momentary escapes, often delays the healing journey and increases emotional detachment.

2. The Role of Online Support Communities

Healing through Digital Spaces: More people are now finding healing in digital spaces, whether it's in online therapy, forums, or support groups. In these virtual communities, people often feel safer than in person, as there's no immediate face-to-face vulnerability. For those who are still reluctant to open up in a physical space, these platforms provide a sense of anonymity that makes it easier to express emotions. It can be a powerful first step in starting the healing process, offering support where it feels inaccessible in the real world.

3. Therapy and Technology

Telehealth and Virtual Therapy: The rise of online therapy has made it more accessible than ever for individuals to seek professional help. Whether due to geographic barriers, time constraints, or the comfort of being in one's own space, telehealth has removed many of the obstacles that prevent people from seeking therapy. Virtual therapy allows people to engage in their healing process at their own pace, creating an accessible option for those who need it most.

Self-Help Apps: Along with virtual therapy, the increasing popularity of self-help apps is also aiding those on the healing journey. Apps designed for mindfulness, mood tracking, and even trauma-informed care are becoming valuable resources. They provide users with tools to track their progress, practice grounding techniques, and access coping strategies in times of crisis. These apps offer a sense of control and provide immediate support when traditional resources may not be available.

4. The Pressure of Always Being "On"

Constant Availability: In both personal and professional realms, technology has made it almost impossible to escape the feeling of constantly being available. With constant notifications, emails, and work demands, the pressure to always be "on" is overwhelming. For individuals already struggling with trauma, this relentless connectivity can worsen emotional burnout. The inability to disconnect from work or personal obligations can lead to a sense of emotional depletion.

There's no space to recover, rest, or recharge, which deepens the cycle of stress, anxiety, and trauma.

Expectation of Response: The demand for immediate responses, whether it's from work, family, or social media, only intensifies the pressure. The longer we remain in this cycle of constant availability, the more we disconnect from ourselves and our ability to prioritize our emotional health. This pressure can leave trauma survivors feeling even more isolated, as they often don't have the time or energy to address their pain. Over time, this can lead to exhaustion, resentment, and burnout.

5. The Silent Suffering of Digital Burnout

Digital Exhaustion: Just as emotional and physical burnout can overwhelm us, digital burnout has become a growing issue. The constant flood of information, virtual interactions, and demands from social media can leave people feeling mentally drained and disconnected. For those already struggling with trauma, this sense of detachment only deepens the emotional burden. People become exhausted not just from their real-world obligations, but from the pressure to keep up in the digital world as well. This constant overstimulation can make it difficult to focus, process emotions, or engage in self-care. It exacerbates feelings of isolation and contributes to the trauma survivor's emotional exhaustion.

Disconnection from Self: The more we engage in the digital world, the further we move away from ourselves. This disconnection from our physical and emotional needs only prolongs the healing process. When we're constantly plugged in, we don't allow ourselves the space to process, rest, or recover. This is where the digital paradox becomes dangerous. It connects us with the world, but it also disconnects us from ourselves.

Conclusion: Living Authentically Every Day

As we've explored throughout this book, unmasking isn't about tearing everything down overnight. It's more like a renovation. A deliberate, layered process of redesigning the life you live to reflect the truth of who you are. One choice at a time. One layer at a time.

Living authentically is the blueprint we've been building toward. Not perfection. Not performance. But truth. And like any solid structure, it starts with a strong foundation: the willingness to stop hiding and to stand in who you truly are.

Authenticity doesn't require you to demolish everything at once. It asks you to examine the framework. What beliefs, behaviors, or roles are load-bearing, and which ones were added over time for appearance or protection? What needs to be reinforced, and what needs to be let go?

This is the real work of designing a life that holds you, not just impresses others.

The core message here is simple but powerful: *You don't have to keep living inside walls you've outgrown.*

Authenticity is not a destination; it's a practice. A daily recalibration. A series of design choices that reflect your inner truth, not just external expectations.

It shows up in your morning routines, in the way you speak your needs, in the boundaries you honor, and in the risks, you take to be seen more fully. It means permitting yourself to take up space as you are, not just the polished, "put together" version of you that others are used to seeing.

And yes, it's uncomfortable at times. Construction always is.

Some days, you'll want to revert to old blueprints, the ones that kept you safe but small. You'll question if your truth is too much or not enough. You'll wonder if it's easier to keep pretending. But remember this:

Every mask you remove gives you a clearer view of your true design.

The courage to live authentically isn't about being fearless. It's about being honest. And that honesty is what creates rooms in your life where others can meet you. Not just admire the exterior, but step inside and truly connect.

You've already started the build. You've examined the architecture of your pain, rewritten old blueprints, and reclaimed your tools. Now, the challenge is to live within what you've designed, staying rooted in the structure you've begun to create.

Because that's how we rise.

Not by patching up the facade, but by becoming the architect of our own restoration.

So, ask yourself daily:

What kind of life am I building today?

And is it honest enough to hold the weight of who I truly am?

This is your invitation to stop performing, stop shrinking, stop redesigning yourself to fit someone else's space.

Build what's real.

Build what's strong.

Build what lasts.

You are not starting from scratch.

You are starting from wisdom.

And the world is waiting for what only you can design.

Frequently Asked Questions About Healing

Q: Why does healing feel so slow, even though I'm trying everything?

A: Healing is not a race. It doesn't always happen quickly. It's a deeply personal process that takes time, patience, and persistence. It can be frustrating, especially when you feel like you're doing everything "right" but still aren't seeing immediate results. One thing I've learned along the way is that healing doesn't follow a timeline. It's not something that can be rushed. Healing happens in waves. Sometimes it feels like you're taking steps backward, but remember, the progress is happening even when you can't see it. Celebrate the small wins, like taking a deep breath when you're feeling overwhelmed or reaching out for support when you need it. Every step forward is part of the process, no matter how small.

Q: How do I begin processing emotions I've buried for years?

A: First, acknowledge that it takes courage to begin this work and that you don't have to do it alone. Emotional healing often starts with a willingness to feel what's been buried. The first step is to create a safe space for yourself by journaling, meditating, or seeking support from a trusted therapist. It's important to approach this process with kindness, without expecting instant relief. Processing emotions can be uncomfortable at first, but over time, it can lead to profound healing. A helpful exercise is to sit quietly and ask yourself what emotions you may have been avoiding. Then, allow yourself to feel them without judgment, knowing that it's okay not to have all the answers. Often, the simplest act of acknowledging your feelings can start the healing process.

Q: How do I begin healing when I feel overwhelmed by everything?

A: Starting can be the hardest part, especially when it feels like there's so much to unpack. I've been there myself feeling like everything was piling up, and I didn't know where to begin. The key is to take it one step at a time. It doesn't have to be a grand gesture or a huge decision. Sometimes, just showing up for yourself in small ways is the beginning of healing. Start by acknowledging where you are without judgment, even if that means just sitting in silence for a moment. Take baby steps, whether that's journaling your thoughts, talking to someone you trust, or practicing self-compassion. Healing doesn't have to start with big changes; even the smallest actions lead to profound shifts over time.

Q: How can I keep going when it feels like nothing is changing?

A: When you're in the thick of healing, it can feel like you're stuck in a never-ending cycle, and that can be discouraging. I've experienced that too. But I've learned that even when things feel stagnant, you are still growing. Healing is not always linear, and progress isn't always visible.

What I've found helpful is to stop focusing so much on the end result, and instead, focus on the daily act of showing up for yourself. Sometimes it's enough to make it through the day, or to take a moment to breathe deeply and acknowledge where you are. Remember, every day you choose to keep going, even when it feels like nothing is changing, you are making progress.

Q: How do I find hope in the middle of feeling lost or stuck?
A: I know what it's like to feel lost and stuck, to wonder if hope is something meant for others but not for you. But here's what I want you to know: hope is not always something you find immediately. Sometimes, it's something you have to choose. Even when everything around you feel dark, you can still choose to take that first step. Hope can be as simple as holding onto the belief that things can be different, even if you can't see how yet. It doesn't have to be a giant leap; it's the quiet faith that tomorrow holds the possibility of something better. Trust that healing is a journey, not a destination, and each step, no matter how small, moves you closer to the hope you seek.

Q: How can I manage feelings of guilt or shame associated with my healing?
A: Guilt and shame are common emotions that many people experience during the healing process, particularly when they feel like they've "let others down" or are struggling to live up to expectations. These feelings are often rooted in perfectionism, and it's important to remember that healing is not about being perfect; it's about being human.

One therapeutic approach that can be helpful here is Cognitive Behavioral Therapy (CBT), which helps you challenge and reframe negative thought patterns. Ask yourself: What evidence do I have for these feelings of guilt or shame? Often, when you examine them critically, you'll find that they're based on unrealistic standards. Self-compassion and mindfulness can also be powerful tools for releasing guilt and shame. Allow yourself to be imperfect and recognize that healing is a process that takes time and patience.

Q: What if I don't feel ready to talk about my pain with others?
A: It's completely okay not to feel ready to share your pain with others, and you should never feel pressured to do so before you feel comfortable. It's also important to remember that talking about your pain is not the only way to heal. Healing can occur through writing, self-reflection, or creative expression, whichever allows you to process your emotions safely and privately. The goal is not to rush yourself into vulnerability, but to build trust with yourself gradually. When you're ready, reaching out for professional support, such as seeing a therapist, can help guide you through the process of expressing your pain in healthy, manageable ways.

Q: How do I support a loved one who is going through silent suffering?
A: Supporting someone who is silently suffering can be challenging because they may not always show signs of distress. As a Licensed Professional Counselor, I always emphasize the importance of creating

a non-judgmental, open space for the person to feel heard and validated. Sometimes, just saying, "I'm here for you, whenever you're ready to talk," can make a huge difference. Encourage them to express themselves in a way that feels comfortable for them, whether through writing, art, or even physical activity. Be patient; don't push them to talk before they're ready. Remind them that seeking professional support, such as therapy, can provide a safe space for them to process their feelings.

Q: How can I heal while feeling stuck in a cycle of negative thoughts?

A: Negative thought cycles are a common barrier to healing but can be interrupted with practice. One technique I often use in therapy is mindfulness, which helps break the cycle of rumination by bringing attention to the present moment. Practicing mindfulness can be as simple as focusing on your breath for a few minutes each day or grounding yourself by paying attention to your surroundings. Additionally, reframing negative thoughts is an essential strategy. Ask yourself, is this thought rooted in reality, or is it just my mind spiraling? Challenge those negative thoughts by considering more balanced or positive perspectives. Therapy can also help you address the underlying causes of these thought patterns, which often stem from past trauma or deep-seated fears.

A Final Thought:

Healing isn't a straight line. There will be moments of struggle, doubt, and darkness,

And that's okay. Every step you take toward healing, no matter how small or challenging, is a victory in itself. You don't need to have all the answers or be perfect. What matters most is that you keep moving forward with grace, courage, and kindness toward yourself. The journey ahead may be long, but you are never truly alone. You are deserving of healing, hope, and the peace that awaits on the other side.

www.ingramcontent.com/pod-product-compliance
Lightning Source LLC
Chambersburg PA
CBHW070937180426
43192CB00039B/2304